Llyfrgell Sir POWYS Coun
Llandrindod Wells LD

powys.gov.uk/lib

D0997272

Powys

37218 00518157 8

The VW Camper Van

The
VW Camper Van
A Biography

Mike Harding

First published in Great Britain
2013 by Aurum Press Ltd
74–77 White Lion Street
London N1 9PF
www.aurumpress.co.uk

Copyright © Mike Harding 2013

Mike Harding has asserted his moral right to be identified as the author
of this work in accordance with the Copyright, Designs and
Patents Act 1988.

All rights reserved. No part of this book may be reproduced or utilised
in any form or by any means, electronic or mechanical, including
photocopying, recording or by any information storage and retrieval
system, without permission in writing from Aurum Press Ltd.

Page 115: 'Meeting Mr Miandad' © Sony/ATV Music Publishing LLC

Every effort has been made to trace the copyright holders of material
quoted in this book. If application is made in writing to the publisher, any
omissions will be included in future editions.

A catalogue record for this book is
available from the British Library.

ISBN 978 1 84513 605 5

1 3 5 7 9 10 8 6 4 2
2013 2015 2017 2016 2012

Typeset in Perpetua by SX Composing DTP, Essex
Printed and bound by CPI Group (UK) Ltd, Croydon, CR0 4YY

'I gave her my trust and bought her a microbus'

The Grateful Dead

Contents

Introduction

So admired for your body
So bewitching are your eyes
So beguiling on the split scene
Every chance to win first prize
With your never ending story
In the south west having fun
Gently cruising in the slow lane
Never fast enough for some

'Keep on Turning the Wheel'
Fairport Convention

THERE CAN SCARCELY BE A more iconic vehicle than the VW Camper Van. Whether it's the early 'Splitty' or one of the later 'Bays', the rounded, friendly shape of what was, in its first conception, a simple workhorse and goods carrier is recognised all over the world. The 'Bus' or 'Kamper' or 'Vee Dub' (to give it just a few of its names) has never failed to raise a smile amongst the general population, and at the same time has generated what is the next best thing to religious fervour amongst its fans.

It's hard to define exactly what it is that makes the VW Camper Van so special and inspires such loyalty. There are, after all, many other types of vans and campers that have rolled on and off the rolling roads of history like the Citroën Nomad, the Commer Highwayman or the Bedford Dormobile, but none of them seems, to enjoy the same fanatical loyalty or affection as the Camper Van. What rolled off the assembly lines in Wolfsburg, Germany as the VW Type 2 Transporter, a simple 'box on wheels' aimed at satisfying the need in a ruined postwar Europe for a simple load carrier, is now known and loved all across the world. I have been amazed while researching this book at the number of people who, when I mentioned the subject, have said to me, 'We used to have a VW Camper when we were first married, we had ever so many holidays in it, it was wonderful. We only sold it in the end because the kids got too big for it,' or who, like my old accountant, Mike, said, 'We had one of those. A gang of us bought it when we were students and went all the way to Marrakech in it.' So many people have their own Camper Van stories to tell, whether of simple holidays in the English countryside, months away in the south of France or epic journeys across the Hindu Kush. What started life as nothing more exciting than a flatbed runabout in a bombed-out German factory has taken millions of people on voyages of discovery where they often discover more about what is going on inside their own souls than in the outside world.

The Hopi Indians of the American south-west have a proverb, 'The journey is our religion', and, in a way, the journeys people have made in and with their 'Dubs' have often been quasi-religious experiences that have changed them in ways subtle and not so subtle.

It might seem strange to see the spirit of writers like John Muir, George Borrow, Henry Thoreau, Patrick Leigh Fermor and Jack Kerouac in a book about something which has been called, 'a tin tent on wheels', but I believe that the gentle but pervasive whiff of revolt and anarchy that I sense in the air along with the smell of Campinggaz and frying bacon at various Dubmeets and vanfests, comes from the same spirit of rebellion and individualism that these writers celebrated.

Kerouac in *On the Road* and *The Dharma Bums* rejoiced in the road itself, the freewheeling life that turned its back on what had been packaged and marketed as the American Dream with its 2.4 kids and walk-in fridges. Instead he set off riding the rails or hitchhiking down the highway with a sunburned thumb, pursuing the dream of the free individual, the wanderer, the seeker after truth. The earlier writings of the outdoors men like Thoreau and the 'Beats' like Kerouac later come to fruition in the 'hippy' movement of the sixties, and it was of course that very movement that took the Camper Van to its heart. Even today the VW Camper Van, with its universal peace symbol and adorned with hand-painted flowers and pentagrams, is something many people identify with the sixties and the Woodstock generation.

I suspect that many of my fellow Camper Van nuts would object to being likened to old-fashioned socialists, hippies, Beats and anarchists like Kerouac and Ken Kesey but I think it is possible to see in today's Camper Van owners, with their festivals and their Dub clubs and their long-distance travels, the same spirit that infused the radicals and the hippies. In the way they travel, the way they decorate their vans, the way (more importantly) they refuse to scrap them – recycling everything, rebuilding them and in some cases almost resurrecting them – the Vee Dubbers are sticking two fingers up at the mass-consumption world that would turn us all into label-hungry spendaholics. Every kid that hits the open road heading for a campsite with his or her mum and dad is another kid that isn't stuck upstairs alone in the bedroom playing on their games module while their parents sit downstairs watching *Celebrity Water Skiing* or *Celebrity Cooks' Nudist Camp* or whatever it is the ratings chasers are spewing out over the networks that particular week. Sitting outside your Camper Van while the kids make sandcastles may be a small vote for freedom, but as Mahatma Gandhi pointed out when he crossed the O'Connor Pass In County Kerry, Ireland in his Splitty, if you add all those small votes together you get enough to give one or two politicians loose bowels. Many of us may love the Camper Van because it symbolises freedom and the open road, but there is also something in the van's very design that seems to generate affection in people. It's not too fanciful to say that the Camper Van is probably one of the most pleasant and friendly-looking vehicles ever made. The Morris Minor 1000 and the old Austin Healey 'Frogeye' Sprite seem to me to be the only British models that come close to it in the cuddle stakes.

Perhaps much of the love that people feel for the Camper Van is something to do with the van's face, because from the very first, what you see when you look at a Splitty or a Bay is a pleasant, friendly creature. The smooth, rounded body is finished off with a smiling bumper, two headlamp eyes and either the v-nose of the Splitty or the bulbous nose of the Bay Window's spare wheel. The VW Transporter van was the kind of vehicle that said, right from when it first rolled off the assembly line in Wolfsburg, 'I am the future', but it said it in a smiling and companionable way. If you look at some of the early advertising graphics by the artist Bernd Reuters, you can see that the van, particularly the Microbus Deluxe version, was not unlike the Dymaxion designed by Buckminster Fuller – his futuristic car was shaped like every schoolboy's dream of the science fiction worlds to come.

As a child I was a huge fan of the *Eagle* comic and in particular of one of its characters, Dan Dare, Pilot of the Future. Created and drawn by Frank Hampson, an ex-RAF pilot from Southport, Lancashire, the world of Dan Dare was a futuristic, modernist one in which smooth-lined, rocket ships and vehicles propelled themselves round cities of the world to come that were all glass and steel, curving lines and rounded edges. Looking at some of the earlier advertising for the VW Kombi Westfalia, the top-of-the-line VW Camper Van conversion, it is not hard to imagine Dan Dare and Digby, his tubby Yorkshire companion, driving one. I like to think of them in retirement, a trillion light years away from the Mekon and his floating commode, zooming along English country lanes on a camping holiday, khaki shorts neatly pressed and hanging up in the wardrobe (it's a Westie), fridge full of India Pale Ale and Yorkshire pudding mix, their fishing rods, banjo and concertina in the back – they are ready for anything.

Chapter 1

Making Rain in a Panel Van

When your sisters lay a rusting
And your brothers failed the test
You were playing happy families
Such a cut above the rest
Traveled miles in old money
As gallons poured into your tank
Breaking down wasn't funny
Had to sit out on the bank

'Keep on Turning the Wheel'
Fairport Convention

THE FIRST VW TRANSPORTER to enter my life, and the one that has stayed in my mind ever since, was a sealing-wax red, Splitty Panel Van. This played a Jekyll and Hyde role as rock 'n' roll wheels to a load of spotty teenagers during the night, and ferried bolts of cloth around the cotton mills and warehouses of Lancashire during the day. It was 1961, and the rock 'n' roll group that used the van for transporting their amps, drums and guitars (and occasionally for sleeping in) was called The Manchester Rainmakers. This was to distinguish us from another group on the scene at the time called The Warrington Rainmakers, and, I suppose, any other Rainmakers that might have been knocking round the northern rock 'n' roll world of the sixties. (The Giggleswick Rainmakers? The Oswaldtwistle Rainmakers?) The name came, I believe, from a 1956 film called *The Rainmaker* which told the story of a spinster in a drought-stricken, American small town who falls in love with a charlatan who claims he can make it rain. Naturally it all ends terribly. She should have moved to Manchester where it might not rain all the time but where the people do have webbed feet and the buses give lifeboat drill before setting off.

I suppose somebody must have thought that The Rainmakers was a striking name for a band that came from the Rainy City, and I suppose that same somebody thought it was a good idea to have the band photographed holding umbrellas. I have to admit that, in those days, I was a callow youth and was so in awe of rock 'n' roll that I would have joined any band, even if it had been called The Eccles Existentialists or Storm Damage and the Rocky Foundations, and would have posed standing on my head in a bucket of treacle if they'd asked me.

The previous band I'd been in, The Stylos (named after a shoe shop), didn't have a group van; we used to get lifts to our gigs in the rhythm guitarist's Uncle Ken's Morris Minor Traveller, which was a sort of Elizabethan half-timbered bijou dwelling on wheels. I never quite understood the half-timbering; perhaps it was a harking back to an imagined bucolic past when men wore codpieces and were called Oliver, and women were buxom and called Mistress Moll. Perhaps it was simply a natural result of the English love of suburbia – in which case the car should have had a garden gnome on the bonnet like the flying lady on the Rolls-Royce. Whatever it was, ours was the only group transport with a priest hole and an oubliette and which died, in the end, not from engine failure but from death watch beetle. Many's the mile I travelled lying on blankets in the back of the Traveller on top of three amps and a drum kit as Uncle Ken drove round the backstreets of Salford or Oldham, teeth clamped on his pipe, nose to the wheel, looking for the Luxor Club, Hulme; the Talk of the North, Eccles; or Caesar's Palace, Collyhurst. Most of the clubs we played in were converted billiard halls or cinemas; dark, damp places with glitzy stages and outside toilets, and the thing I remember most about them is that they stank of scampi and chips in the basket (the Matterhorn of sophistication in them there days), stale cigarette smoke and even staler beer.

The Stylos were probably the better band, but The Rainmakers had a proper van: a VW Transporter, almost new, and in one of VW's standard liveries – sealing-wax red. Two of us came from Crumpsall, north of Manchester: myself lead guitar and backing vocals, (though I did sing lead vocal on 'The Sheikh of Araby'), and Pete (rhythm guitar, backing vocals and owner of the van). The drummer, bass player and lead singer came from south of the city so they mostly arrived at gigs separately in the bread van belonging to Ricky, the Scouse singer. He was a chirpy bread delivery man during the day and a tight-trousered rock 'n' roll sex bomb at night. He emptied out half a ton of Wonderloaf, sliced Hovis and milk loaves and replaced them with Terry the bass player and Dave the drummer. They usually arrived at the gigs covered in crumbs and smelling delicious, and girls followed them round for the smell of fresh bread alone (I wonder why no one has thought of marketing it as an aftershave).

Our VW had no seats in the back so on the odd occasion when the van was carrying more than us two Crumpsalites, one of us had to lie flat out on the gear as the bus rattled its way over the Pennines to Cleckheaton and Milnrow, or back along the 'A' roads from Blackpool, Matlock, Bolton, Buxton or Leek, all regular gigging towns for us. If we had to transport a crowd, the neddy in the back was usually me. But mostly it was just the two of us: Pete driving and me beside him, dozing off after a hard day of A-level history, and an even harder night of rock 'n' roll. I was only seventeen at the time, and was trying hard to combine a high-flying career as an A-level student at St Bede's RC College in Manchester with a night-time glory job as lead guitarist in one of the north's top rock 'n' roll bands. It was not a very successful spinning of plates, and most of the time I was only half awake, both on stage and in class, where the doings of Luther, Calvin and Zwingli would spool around my head in a dark soup as I tried to focus on a wobbling blackboard and make notes on Justification by Faith while the chord sequences of 'Hog For You Baby' and 'She Was Just Seventeen' ran along as a soundtrack.

At nights I occasionally broke nasal inhalers open and swallowed the impregnated cotton-wool insides because, according to the jazzers and bluesers I knew in Manchester, they contained Benzedrine and would keep you awake. They didn't keep me awake, they just gave me a terrible case of heartburn – which did, in fact, keep me awake, so I suppose they worked in a way.

From time to time on those long, tedious journeys back from gigs, I would be woken from my dreamy slumbers by Pete screaming, 'Talk to me! Talk to me! I'm falling asleep at the bleedin' wheel!' in a voice that almost shattered the windows and certainly didn't do much for my nerves. There wasn't anything like the amount of traffic you find on the roads in this congested twenty-first century so it was quite easy to nod off as the six-volt van with lights as powerful as two jam-jars full of glow-worms trundled along on deserted moor-land roads at fifty miles an hour.

Many years later in Austin, Texas, while wearing my BBC Radio 2 hat, I interviewed Ray Benson, the lead singer of the band Asleep At The Wheel and, as he was talking into the microphone about Texas Swing and Bob Wills and His Texas Playboys, my mind involuntarily went back to those long dark nights of the rock 'n' roll soul, when I kept Pete from falling asleep at the wheel by telling him about the Diet of Worms and the Gutenberg Bible as we crossed that narrow and forbidding road over the bogs and marshes of Saddleworth Moor, or made our lonely way home from Southport by endless fields of potatoes and cabbages. Thinking back on those days from the vantage point of my anecdotage I suppose it was quite apt to be talking about Lutheranism to a knackered rhythm guitarist in a van that was conceived in Lower Saxony, Germany.

I had a go at driving the van once or twice (even though I didn't have a licence and hadn't passed my test) and found it really easy to drive. It was much nicer than the Ford Thames that I later drove for my Uncle Harry when I worked in his carpet shop. That had a steering column gear change, a footbath in the driver's side when it rained, and was a complete pig to start if the temperature fell to lower than that enjoyed by your average African desert republic. The VW, on the other hand, had a smart dashboard, an air-cooled engine and started every time, no matter what the weather had decided to do. It pulled like a train and was warm and comfy – too much so for Pete on those long drives home.

During the day, when I was not at school, I would give Pete a hand to stack all the amps and speakers and microphone stands in his mother's front room in Crumpsall, and we would set off to huge warehouses like India House and other grand relics of Cottonopolis. There we would load the van with bolts of cloth and take them out to the finishers. The death rattle of King Cotton could just about be heard in the streets of the north, and as the old king wheezed and gasped his life away in the few remaining mills, we made a couple of quid a day carting the last of Lancashire's cotton to the dyers and printers. I was always amazed at how much stuff we could get in the van and doubly amazed at how she seemed to be able to carry it all without falling apart.

I couldn't say that those rock 'n' roll days in the VW left me hopelessly in love with the Panel Van, but it gave me a fondness for the old girl and a healthy respect for the model. Even as a mechanical illiterate I could see that the bus was just about as perfect as any light Transporter of its time could be. It was certainly auto-bahns ahead of the Surbiton bungalow on wheels that was the Morris Minor Traveller; it was comfy and reliable and it had style by the bucketload.

After a year or so I left the group, and the world of rock 'n' roll, and immersed myself in taking exams, getting thrown out of school, getting married, getting a job on the buses and the dustbins and any other job I could find while bringing up a family. While doing all of that I turned from rock 'n' roll to folk and began another life travelling the country, from Stirling to Southend and from Ecclefechan to Exeter, playing folk music in the upstairs rooms of pubs. My vehicles of choice ranged from a hand-painted maroon minivan with a racing steering wheel and Weber twin carbs that had once been green and used to take a painter and decorator about, to a 1300cc VW Beetle which was also the family car and ran four people and a dog around the Yorkshire Dales.

It was Whitby Folk Festival, way back in the late sixties, that gave me my 'Road to Damascus' moment. I saw a couple sitting outside their lovely Westfalia Splitty in the afternoon sun supping tea while their children played on the beach and, like St Paul, I saw the light. Seeing the light and turning it into a tin tent on wheels are two different things, and, for various reasons, owning a VW Camper became both something of a secret dream and a family joke. It was a symbol of freedom and endless possibilities to me, but to the rest of my family it was a sign that inside this middle-aged fart there was a long-buried but now reborn hippy fart struggling to get out. The dream eventually turned into an obsession, and I began to crave a Camper Van of my own. I filled my bookshelves with books on Splittys and Bays, and all the nooks and crannies of the house held VW Camper Vans in the shape of tea-light holders, money boxes and fridge magnets. I even bought two books on restoring and maintaining Camper Vans, illustrated with hand-drawn images in the style of Robert Crumb and the other California underground comic artists. This meant I knew all about installing twin carbs and welding on a new battery pan, even though I hadn't got a van and, judging by the way I was shaping up, hadn't the vaguest chance of getting one.

I had Camper Vanitis very bad. In fact I had become

that most pitiful of beings: the Camper Van manqué obsessive. This amused my friends and family, and was mostly looked on simply as a powerful but harmless obsession – like stamp collecting or trainspotting. For more years than I want to remember, I pulled up whenever I saw a Camper Van at the side of the road and confused complete strangers with inane questions about their little four-wheeled palaces. I realised that all this was becoming very serious indeed when, at the Sidmouth Folk Festival one summer, I bored the crust off two polite women in an Early Bay (Devon conversion) by chuntering on about how much I loved Camper Vans. They had just started making breakfast, but recognising me as a Camper Van nut they very kindly were the acme of patience. They smiled and nodded politely at the gibbering fool in shorts and T-shirt standing outside their open door, wittering on and on and on like the Ancient Mariner about Westies and Danburys, until their bacon caught fire under the grill and they had to flap it out with tea towels.

After that I stopped bothering people, though I didn't stop looking, and spent hours online searching out Campers for sale on sites like G'day Campers and Dubs4sale. I found a good few that I liked, but they were often too far away for me to go and see or, if I did get serious, were already sold. But I still kept looking, even though friends still laughed and went on buying me VW memorabilia for birthdays and Christmas and kept asking me when I was going to get a real one. This continued, quite literally, for years. I once drove all the way from the Yorkshire Dales to Gloucestershire to look at the Danbury workshops there (to save you looking, they've moved to Bristol now) because I'd just been filming a pilot for TV and had used a friend's Danbury Rio as my transport (this was years before it became something of a televisual cliché). But still, for one reason and another, I didn't take the plunge.

I even ended up in Wolfsburg, the home of the VW, and drooled over the classic vans in the museum there. It was 2005, and I'd been invited to open an exhibition of work by a German artist friend of mine, Joachim Boske. Joe, as he is more generally known, is one of the most amazing painters that I have come across. I first met him on the streets of Clifden, Connemara many moons ago when I was in town shopping (I have a small cottage on the coast, just north of the town). Joe has lived in the west of Ireland for more than thirty years now. Much of his art is inspired by the western fringes of that country, and his paintings have become extremely collectible. As one of Saxony's most famous artist sons, the VW company decided to honour him with an exhibition in their famous Autostadt, and a gang of musicians, painters and

poets from the west of Ireland made the journey over
to Wolfsburg for the opening. The day before, we were
taken on a VIP tour of the VW factory in an open-top
stretch Beetle, our guide pointing out the shell- and
bullet-holes still there from the Allied bombing of the
Second World War. I couldn't help but wonder, as we
looked up at the holes, whether my father's Lancaster
hadn't perhaps been responsible for a few of them.
After the tour of the factory we were shown around
the museum, which for me was like dying and going to
motor car heaven, and my jaw was on my chest most
of the time. From a sawn-in-half modern Beetle to one
of the very first Type 1 Cabriolets there was everything
a VW fanatic would want to see. However, plead as I
would, they refused to let me take one of the early VW
Panel Vans home with me.

That afternoon, sitting before a few pints in an old bar
in the town centre, I met an elderly man called Harry
who had worked for VW for more than fifty years. He
spoke perfect English, and among other things had
run VW Ireland in the early days of the firm's expan-
sion into the rest of Europe. He told me how, in 1945,
he had set out from the factory to find the advancing
Americans who were, he said, 'lost on their advance'
and were stuck at the canal a few kilometres to the west.
The Russian slave labourers who had been working in

the factory were without supervision, the guards keeping them under control having fled, and now they were running amok all around the town and the surrounding countryside, looting and raping. Harry found the lost Americans and led them into the town, then on into the factory, sitting astride the barrel of a Sherman tank smoking a big Cuban cigar. It's interesting to think that, if Harry hadn't led the Americans there first, it is more than possible that Russian troops might have gained control of the area and the Beetle would have become a Trabant or a Škoda.

It was after my visit to the Autostadt that things finally came to a head between me and the VW Camper. I realised if I didn't do something drastic I would remain a Camper Van bachelor until I popped my clogs and they fitted me with a wooden overcoat, so I stopped browsing the web, took out my cheque book and made a huge manic lunge into the unknown – Preston, to be more precise.

She was lurking like a Lancashire strumpet down a back alley in a narrow, terraced, red-brick street in that desperately over-trafficked town: a 2001 Type 2 Bay Window, Brazilian-made, Danbury import. With a hot-orange lower and off-white upper, she winked at me once and I was lost. Her authentic, classic body had come off the original presses, but she was modern made with a 1600cc engine and metalwork that was perfect except for a couple of minor rust spots. In theory at least, I was buying a modern version of a classic, and she needed, it seemed, nothing doing to her. (Haven't we all been there?) She was a bit shabby, but who was I to complain? I was no oil painting myself. A scrawl of pen on NatWest paper, three days of waiting for the cheque to clear and she was mine.

I drove her home one wet and blustery winter's night as the light was failing, making my way along the Ribble Valley towards my home in the Yorkshire Dales, taking it nice and easy as we got to know one another. The gear lever seemed to be further away than I remembered, and the steering wheel seemed very big after the little thing I was used to on my Toyota Rav 4, but eventually we made it back to Ribblesdale. I took a shedload of photographs of her the next morning and emailed them to friends all round the world. Almost all of them emailed me back to say I should have done it years ago, and then asked me what she was called.

I hadn't thought about a name but realised now that of course she had to have one. My friends, the folk singer Martin Simpson and his partner Kit Bailey, have a lovely little daughter called Molly, and Molly is also the name of one of my grandsons', Felix and Toby's favourite characters in the *Thomas the Tank Engine* stories – so

Molly she became. The afternoon of the next day I took Molly for a ride, setting off from my house and heading over to Bowland Knotts on the edge of the Bowland Fells. I parked up on the tops, completely alone as the sun sank into the west and long shadows crept across the hills in front of me. Then I made myself a cup of tea on the stove, and sat in the van watching the sun set behind the wild Lancashire moors. I felt that at long last, 'Poop Poop!' like Toad in *The Wind in the Willows*, it was the open road for me. Of course there were a few things wrong with Molly, and I have ended up spending a few bob getting her resprayed and fitted with a new radio, Weber twin carbs and other such stuff, but that's a story for another time. Since that afternoon I have trundled Molly all over the place: fishing trips to the Eden Valley; music sessions at the highest pub in England, the Tan Hill; folk festivals on the Fylde coast and the Langdale Valley, and Vee Dub festivals in the deep south – and so far we haven't fallen out.

Chapter 2

The Lancashire Lad and the Doodling Dutchman, or How Volkswagen Almost Never Was

So HOW WAS IT THAT a war-crippled Germany managed to produce two of the most iconic vehicles in the world: the Beetle and the Type 2 Camper Van? Was it accident? Fate? Kismet? Omar Khayyám's 'moving finger'? Perhaps it was all of these things. But the kismet had a precedent, and though what you are about to read next might seem a diversion, it is not.

In 1903 two remarkable men met in the newly built Midland Hotel, Manchester. Amongst the many American cotton traders from Savannah and New Orleans who had crossed the Atlantic to deal in raw cotton and were sitting chatting and smoking in the sumptuous restaurant of the Midland Railway's newest luxury hotel, were two Englishmen, Charles Stewart Rolls and Frederick Henry Royce. Three years after that meeting those two men founded Rolls-Royce, a not inconsiderable marque in the history of motoring.

In a similar way the meeting of three equally remarkable men in the less salubrious setting of a bombed-out motor works in Saxony just after the Second World War led to both the birth of another iconic vehicle – the Volkswagen Type 2 or Panel Van – and also, as a result of the massive popularity of both the Type 2 and its older brother the Type 1, or Beetle, to the postwar resurrection of the Germany economy and therefore the whole nation. The three men who met in that war-damaged car factory were a British army officer, Major Ivan Hirst; a Dutch car dealer, Ben Pon; and a German automobile engineer, Heinrich Nordhoff.

Each of the three men had an important part to play in the story of Volkswagen. It was Ivan Hirst who almost single-handedly kept the factory alive in the first years of the Allied occupation; it was Ben Pon who first came up with the idea of the light Transporter vehicle that eventually became the Type 2; and it was Professor Nordhoff who had the determination and vision that made not just the Type 1 Beetle but the Type 2 Transporter amongst the best-selling vehicles of all time.

Ivan Hirst is one of the key figures in the whole Volkswagen story. Not only was he a military man and a highly skilled engineer, he had imagination and empathy, and saw that the ruined factory that had been placed in his care was capable, with repair and organisation, of providing both work and hope for the people of the destroyed country about him. It was truly fortunate that Hirst was an engineer. British army officers sent in to manage war-ravaged Germany after 1945 came from all walks of life. Some were professional soldiers who knew how to tell men how to fight battles but not very much about anything else; others were not military men at all but came from all sorts of professions: medicine, the law, accountancy, architecture and even the liberal arts. That they sent an engineer to the Saxony motor works was pure fate. If a classicist with a degree in Latin and Greek had been sent to look after the ruined VW car factory in 1945 and told to 'basically just sit there', as Ivan Hirst was told to do, he may well have done just that – sat there and waited until somebody came along, took one look at the works, dismantled the plant and presses, and shipped them back to Coventry or Oxford as war reparation.

The massive KdF-Stadt (Kraft-durch-Freude – Strength Through Joy) motor car factory was built by the Nazi Party before the Second World War in meadowland in Fallersleben, Lower Saxony, taking as its model the great Henry Ford works in America. KdF had originally been a Nazi leisure organisation, founded in the 1930s, dedicated to sports and culture. By 1936 it had turned itself into an industrial labour organisation and, as such, began to build not just its own factories but ocean-going liners designated as cruise ships. These were not for the enjoyment of the upper classes, but for the workers of post-Depression Germany. Like the liners, the factory was an important totemic building for the Nazis; not only was it the largest auto plant under a single roof anywhere in the world, but it was built and managed solely by the KdF sector of the party. The Fallersleben works, funded completely by Nazi money, had been constructed to turn out a car that would be within the financial grasp of any worker. The family saloon car was commissioned by Hitler and was designed by a little-known independent contractor called Ferdinand Porsche. By 1937 Porsche had built three prototypes and, with typical German thoroughness and precision, had tested them over 100,000 miles. Hitler, impatient at the German car industry's lack of interest in producing the car, decided instead to build his own factory, which is how the KdF works came into being.

The car was originally simply called the Type 1, but soon came to be known as the 'Beetle' because of its scarab-like shape. It was Hitler who named the car the Volkswagen – the 'People's Car' – and his great hope was that, ultimately, every family in Germany that wanted one should be able to afford one. With this in mind, as part of his long-term plan for his thousand-year Reich, he built the autobahns. These fast, modern roads were designed not just for the rapid movement of troops but also to take his new People's Car. Hitler regarded the Beetle as his own personal baby and kept a keen eye on the vehicle's development; any search on the internet will bring up numerous pictures and film clips of Hitler and other high-ranking Nazis riding in or poring admiringly over VWs.

Yet it transpired that, in spite of all the propaganda and all the newsreel footage, the VW Beetle didn't go into full production until after the war. The war began in September 1939, and the first Beetle came off the assembly line on 15 August 1940. Among the first owners were Hitler himself and Hermann Goering, his deputy, but the factory would soon be switched over from the production of cars to military vehicles. Once Germany invaded Poland in 1939, the country was on a war footing, and during the whole of the conflict only 600 cars were made, and almost all of those went to high-ranking Nazi officials. Fun things would have to wait until Hitler had finished his job of building his Greater Germany.

During the six years of the war the Fallersleben works turned from making People's Cars to the manufacture of light military vehicles, in particular the Kübelwagen (literally 'bucket-seat car', a German version of the American jeep) and the Schwimmwagen which was, quite simply, a water-going Kübelwagen. Both vehicles were based on the original Porsche-designed Type 1 Beetle and kept its distinctive features, revolutionary for the time, of full independent suspension and a rear-mounted air-cooled engine. Both the Kübelwagen and the Schwimmwagen served in every theatre of the war, and captured vehicles never failed to impress the Allied engineers who looked at them. They were the epitome of German design and manufacture, brilliantly engineered and completely reliable. As well as vehicles the factory also turned out stoves to keep soldiers warm on the Russian front and was never, as some writers have claimed, involved in the production of parts for V2 rockets. Nonetheless the factory was an important part of the German war effort and, in the terrible carpet-bombing raids that marked the last years of the Second World War, the town and factory were all but destroyed by the bombs of the USAF and the RAF. By 1945 65 per cent of the works was in ruins, and the rear of Hall 1 housed the remains of a massive American bomber.

In a way the state of the factory in 1945 could be seen as a symbol of the condition of Germany itself, because, like the works, the country had been pretty much laid waste. It is hard for those of us who have not had to live through total war and total defeat to understand what Germany was like in the months following the collapse of the Third Reich: the currency was worthless; the government was in chaos; most major cities were in ruins; there was little transport of any kind; and the citizenry were confused, depressed and in total shock. Government of every kind, national and local, had broken down to the extent that there was not even a police force. Many German business managers had either fled the country or been imprisoned as Nazis so the private sector was as much a basket case as civic society. Gas, electricity and sewerage had been destroyed, and bands of slave labourers and displaced persons were, according to a BBC Home Service documentary of the time, roaming the deserted streets of the cities and towns robbing, looting and murdering. The slave labourers, originally brought in from conquered countries such as Poland, Czechoslovakia, Hungary, Yugoslavia, Italy and Holland to serve the Nazi war machine, had suddenly found themselves liberated. Many of them had nowhere to go, and some of them, particularly those from the east, preferred life in a defeated Germany to life behind what Churchill would later call, 'the Iron Curtain'. Amid all this chaos, medicine, food, clothing, fuel and housing were desperately hard to come by, and it was all the Allies could do to keep the population alive and free from any major epidemics.

Oliver Postgate, creator of the children's TV classics *Bagpuss*, *Ivor the Engine* and *Noggin the Nog*, was stationed in Germany in those days doing his National Service as part of the occupying forces. He describes, in his most readable memoir, *Seeing Things*, how even respectable middle-class Germans were struggling to survive and were reduced, in some cases, to thieving and looting simply to stay alive.

Just after midnight, in the pitch dark, we drew up quietly beside the railway yards at the other side of town. I could see nothing except the black silhouette of the sheds. Giff turned the 15cwt so that its nose was pointing into the yard. Then he turned the headlights on. I saw a train of coal trucks on the siding. The chutes had been opened so that the coal had slipped in heaps onto the track. Clambering over the heaps were literally hundreds of people, furtively scooping the coal into baskets and bags. What impressed me was the fact that so many of them were well dressed and that the rucksacks they were stuffing with coal were expensive framed types,

the ones mountain climbers use. Fearing the light they
scuttled round to the dark side. So we came away.

Fallersleben, together with its ruined factory, was initially liberated by the Americans led by Harry astride
his tank, but had been handed over to the British, and
now fell under the BAOR (British Army of the Rhine)
zone of control. The first British officer to venture into
the KdF factory was Lieutenant Colonel John Mackay.
He arrived in the works with his soldiers on 15 May
1945 and found, to his amazement, that the plant was
still operating under the supervision of a small management team and was somehow managing to turn out
around ten Kübelwagens a day. Mackay noticed that all
the vehicles coming off the assembly line were painted
in Afrika Korps sand yellow, even though the war had
been over for some time and the German army hadn't
been anywhere near Africa since 1943. When he asked
why they were still turning out desert patrol cars for a
war that was long over, Mackay was told that they were
doing so because nobody had told them to stop.

Mackay took a good hard look at the factory and the
town that had been built to serve it and realised that
something had to be done, and quickly. In his area of
control alone, as well as the resident German population, there were more than 30,000 ex-slave labourers

and displaced persons. They needed food and they needed something to do, if only for dignity's sake. He set about getting the town back to work.

There were two bodies involved in the rebuilding of the wasteland that was Germany: the Allied armed forces which were still policing the country, making safe arms and minefields and searching out war criminals; and the military government which had taken on the job of governing Germany at all levels. This governing body was made up of a mix of civilian and military officials: solicitors, engineers, accountants, dieticians, teachers, bankers, nurses and other professions. With communist Russia to the east it was felt imperative that Germany was rebuilt as a buffer against the USSR.

The occupying powers had a clear playing field to work on. The country still had, in spite of the Nazi years, an understanding of democracy, and still had the remnants of local civil governance, so, although the British army's task was immensely difficult, it was not utterly impossible. Mackay saw that the factory at Fallersleben was badly damaged but not completely beyond saving. The power station was still functioning, and Hall 1, though it did have the remains of a Flying Fortress in it, was a good site for a repair workshop. Mackay set up a REME (Royal Electrical and Mechanical Engineers) unit in the damaged factory, using British officers and the skilled local workforce to repair American jeeps and British and German military trucks. A few Kübelwagens were also turned out for the British army.

As part of the de-Nazification of Germany, the government of occupation decided to change the name of the town from Fallersleben (the name of the village where the Nazis built their original factory) to Wolfsburg, after Schloss Wolfsburg, the nearby fourteenth-century castle of Count Werner von Schulenberg whose meadowlands had been appropriated by the Nazis for the building of the VW works. The name change, together with a programme of rebuilding, began the slow process of the normalisation of the area. It is now that the really interesting part of the story of Wolfsburg, the VW Beetle and the VW Camper Van truly begins, and it was perhaps only in something like a postwar vacuum of this kind that a story like this could come about.

Saddleworth-born Major Ivan Hirst was one of many British officers overseeing the postwar German reconstruction. After distinguished war service as an infantry captain, he had transferred to REME, and in 1945 found himself in Brussels where he became the works manager of a tank workshop. He soon built up a reputation as both a fine engineer and a good manager of people, and the BAOR posted him to Wolfsburg to take charge of the Volkswagen factory. Hirst had studied optical engineering at Manchester University before the war, and came from an old family of northern watch and clockmakers. Edmund Davies' classic work, *Greater Manchester Clocks and Clockmakers*, records that Hirst Bros. had branches in Oldham, Ashton, Manchester and Birmingham, while other sources mention branches in London and Glasgow. Their most famous clock was the Tameside, named after the River Tame which rises on the Yorkshire-Lancashire border and flows by way of Ashton to join the Mersey and finally the Irish Sea.

Hirst, steeped in engineering, and more importantly infused with a great sense of fair play and of Lancashire 'nous' and spirit, was the very man that the ruined VW works needed to get it back on its feet. He had read about the Volkswagen in pre-war motoring issues of the *Autocar* and, while in Normandy, he had examined some captured Kübelwagens. He had been highly impressed by the air-cooled, light, alloy engine and the independent suspension; interestingly, he now found himself in charge of the factory that made them.

It was a long way from the millstone grit and hills of Lancashire and, as he looked around him, Hirst saw that, though he was used to the destruction of war, things here looked very bleak indeed. He would recall in an interview years later how desperate the situation really was. Below the bedroom of his billet was a small allotment patch where a local man was growing a few potatoes. One night Hirst was woken by scuffling sounds, and looking down could just make out two figures fighting in the gloom. After a while the noises ceased, and in the morning it was found that the man who owned the allotment had discovered somebody stealing his potatoes and had killed him.

Hirst, as well as being a skilled engineer who had a great love of motor cars, was a linguist and a more than capable people manager. Though most writers agree that the part he played in the resurrection of Volkswagen and the future of Germany was immense, he would always play down his role and in fact said, modestly, in 1995, in an interview for television, 'I was just told to go to Fallersleben and basically just sit there.' It would seem that the main reason for sitting there was to wait while decisions were made about the fate of the presses and lathes in the plant. Because the plant had not officially functioned as a motor car factory before the war it was not on the list of industrial works to be revived and, under the terms of postwar reparation, it should have been offered to any of the Allies who wished to bid for it. The Allies, however, were convinced that there was no long-term future for the factory, and in keeping with common practice, in all probability the best and most modern machinery at the plant would have been crated and shipped to England, France, or perhaps Holland. The building itself would probably have been levelled, and the ex-slave workers dispatched to displaced people's camps. But, though he'd been told to 'just sit there', Hirst wasn't the man to just sit anywhere, and in any case what he was sitting on was not, in his judgement, a basket case. The major saw that only 8 per cent of the machinery had been destroyed by the bombing and that only something like 30 per cent of the buildings were in total ruin. Most of the presses and machine tools used in the manufacture of the Beetle had been mothballed and stored in the factory grounds; they were still in working order. He ordered them to be brought back into the works.

With the British car industry still struggling to return to the levels of peacetime working, and many military vehicles now in dire need of repair, both the BAOR and the new governing bodies in Germany desperately needed a fleet of cars. There were several finished, undamaged Volkswagen saloon cars in the factory that had lain there untouched since before the war. Hirst, realising that the plant was just about capable of meeting the British army's need for light vehicles, had one of the cars completely overhauled and serviced and had it painted a military green. He then drove it over to the British army headquarters and showed it to the officers there. The BAOR command, suitably impressed, placed an order with Hirst for 20,000 vehicles of the type officially classed as the 'Volkswagen Type 1' vehicle but which would soon be better known by its nickname, the Beetle. As well as cars the authorities ordered 500 vans and 500 trailers for the post office and 200 khaki-coloured lorries for the BAOR. One simple move, one man with an idea and total commitment to that idea, and the line of history kinks and changes for ever.

And Hirst was only just ahead of the game. There was a famous brigadier roaming Germany in those days who regarded it as his bounden duty to blow things up. It seems that he liked nothing better than to set gelig-nite under something and reduce it to its component parts, particularly if it was a large German factory. His name was Brigadier Blandford Newsome, nicknamed (according to Ivan Hirst) Blasted Nuisance. 'He blew up anything you could see,' Hirst once said. Well he didn't blow up the VW works because, before he could plant his gelignite under it, Hirst had got it up and running and was turning out cars for the occupying forces.

It also has to be said that any appetite which might have still existed for shipping the plant back to England as war reparation diminished after Sir William Rootes, head of the British Rootes Motor Group, famously told

Ivan Hirst, 'If you think you're going to build cars in this place, you're a bloody fool, young man.' Another official British government report stated: 'The vehicle does not meet the fundamental technical requirement of a motor-car . . . it is quite unattractive to the average buyer . . . To build the car commercially would be a completely uneconomic enterprise.' Perhaps because he was in a fairly isolated part of Germany and was off the radar somewhat, and perhaps, more importantly, because he came from that breed of northern non-conformists noted for their dogged individualism, Hirst got on with things his own way.

Some of his methods were not always those you might find in the rule book. For example, when Hirst took the building over he discovered that Russian troops had taken tools and dies from the factory, and that these were now in East Berlin, destined to be moved even further east into Russia. He knew that trying to get them back through official channels would take far too long. The Iron Curtain had not yet been drawn across Europe, but red tape and officialdom would have caused endless delays. He also knew that tooling up and re-jigging to make new dies and tools could take anything up to four years and would probably mean the end of the VW factory. So being a good northern lad with plenty of nous he sent some of the factory personnel over to

East Berlin with a couple of cars loaded with whisky, gin, Players Navy Cut and Woodbine cigarettes. The Russians seemed to think this a fair swap for a load of old machine tools so Hirst got his dies and tools back in return.

With the dies, lathes and presses back in the factory he got the works running again, and by mid-1946 700 workers were turning out more than 1,000 cars a month. By the end of that year they had made 10,000 cars, a remarkable record for a factory that was semi-ruined only the year before. Work only stopped when the most serious blizzards or rainstorms came in through the broken windows and the gaping holes in the factory roof. As a sign that Hirst and the German managers who worked with him had confidence in the future of the company, a number of apprentices were taken on. The work of rebuilding the bombed sections of the factory ran parallel to the regeneration of the assembly line, and bricklaying, glazing and roofing went on as cars were rolling off the presses. Rubble was cleared, windows reinstalled, walls rebuilt and fresh building materials brought in. The little train that had been kept busy before the war shipping in steel and coal was now just as busy shipping out the rubble and returning with loads of cement, glass and bricks.

When asked about the early days of the VW Beetle,

Hirst once replied that his clearest memory was the smell. The car ran well, he said, and was way ahead of any of its competitors in that market, but because of the glue used to fix the headlining (the soft interior roof cloth), on damp days in particular the car used to smell of fish.

There was little enough money to spare in the post-war years but, as Europe began to get back up off its knees, there was a small but growing demand for an economical and versatile car. Hirst, who had rebuilt the old assembly lines and had helped redesign the Beetle, now suddenly found himself overseeing what had turned into a successful motor works. He became a huge enthusiast for the Volkswagen and defended it at every corner against the British authorities. His deeply held view was that the VW works belonged to the German people, and it was his job to build it up and hand it back to them as a healthy, going concern. Working with the design workshop, he constantly improved on the Type 1, re-commissioning tools, power presses and assembly jigs, and setting up a sales and service network.

To improve morale in the works he brought in gram-ophones, amplifiers and speakers, and played music over the PA system into the canteens. He also realised that the old type of labour relations, where the boss was the master and the men the slaves, would not work in the new Europe, so he instigated a works council, something which would later catch on and be found all over Germany. I can't help but feel that if Hirst had been in charge of postwar British industry and had introduced works councils into the British industrial scene, we might have been spared the kind of industrial relations that caused so much bitterness during the last four decades of the twentieth century.

The fact that the car was doing so well did not escape the attention of Ivan Hirst's superior officer, Colonel Charles Radclyffe, the officer with overall responsibility for the factories in the British occupied zone, who told Hirst, according to an interview conducted with him not long before he died, 'I think we've got another world beater here – it's another Model T.'

Chapter 3

A Transporter Without
Compromise

As OUTPUT FROM THE PLANT increased, Major Hirst also began exporting the Beetle, most notably to Holland which was where Ben Pon, the second, important actor in the Volkswagen story would be found.

Hirst had identified one real problem in the plant's working practice: there was no efficient way of moving heavy items such as pressed panels, engines or gearboxes from one end of the factory to the other. For a while they had been getting by with a handful of small electric wagons and some BAOR fork-lifts which the major had requisitioned. But after a while the army wanted their fork-lift trucks back and Hirst was stumped; without transport to move parts around the halls the factory would not be able to operate. For a while it looked as though work would have to stop.

Hirst later recalled thinking, 'We're a car factory, surely we could do something. We'll take the Kübelwagen, put a flat board at one end and a driver's seat, over the engine, at the other.' Together with the people who worked in the experimental shop, Hirst designed a light Transporter that could do the job perfectly. The Plattenwagen (flatbed vehicle) was a small, two-seater, flatbed truck with the driver seated over the engine and transmission at the rear looking forward over the flatbed. Because of the steering design the vehicle had a very small turning circle and was ideal for manoeuvring around the narrow alleyways of the plant. The Plattenwagen became the workhorse of the VW factory, and remained so for some time (in fact the last wagon was not taken out of service until the 1970s).

This handy runabout used the same engine as the Type 1 vehicle or Beetle: the flat four. The beauty of this engine was that, instead of having the standard layout of most engines at the time – four upright cylinders in line above a crankshaft – it had the cylinders lying horizontally in opposing pairs. Things like the oil filter and the distributor were likewise offset and could be accessed easily with the minimum of headroom. All of this reduced the vertical height of the engine and would mean, when it was later adopted for use in the VW Transporter van, that there was a good deal more internal space.

The Plattenwagens were busy running about the factory floor on 23 April 1947 when Bernardus (Ben) Pon walked on stage. Pon, an intelligent and energetic man with a swashbuckling nature and a penchant for large cigars, was a Dutchman who ran his family's car firm in Holland and who had begun building up a relationship with VW before the war. For six years things had been on hold, and now Pon was keen to start importing Beetles into Holland again. Hirst was determined that the new vehicle should be part of a major export business as well as serving the home and military market, and though he sometimes found Pon to be a bit of a nuisance, he did get on with him when it came to business. Pon seems to have been a fairly colourful character, and one version of his first meeting with the military authorities who ran the VW works has him turning up in the full general's uniform of the Dutch army smoking a large cigar in a chauffeur-driven car. He claimed that without this majestic entry nobody would have taken any notice of him. From my own understanding of the military and the motto 'Who dares wins', I think he may well have been right.

Whatever the truth of the matter, Pon became the

main importer of VW Beetles into Holland and was a regular visitor to the Wolfsburg factory. When he turned up there for a business meeting on that April day and saw the Plattenwagens scuttling around the works he immediately saw the potential of the little runabout. The Plattenwagens looked to him like a motorised version of the *bakfiets*, the tricycle delivery vehicles with a box in the front and driver behind, that ran about the towns and cities of his native Holland, and it occurred to him that something similar, in van form, would be ideal as a small commercial vehicle. A light, efficient cargo carrier that was inexpensive and which, like the Beetle, was easy to service and keep on the road was exactly what was needed by firms, both large and small, in a re-capitalised, postwar Europe.

However, when he approached the Dutch authorities with a view to importing the vehicle they turned him down on safety grounds. In their view the Plattenwagen could never be street legal; they wanted the driver seated at the front, not at the back over the engine. Apparently it was fine for the pedal-along trikes to pootle about with the driver stuck at the back but not so fine for something with a 1.2 litre engine powering it. Pon refused to give up on the idea and set about designing a vehicle that used the basic principle of the Plattenwagen but which would satisfy the safety demands of the Dutch authorities. On a sheet of his notebook he sketched out a rough line drawing, so simple as to be almost childlike. It was a profile view of a smooth-prowed van. The driver and passenger seats were at the front, over the axle; the engine was at the rear, likewise over the axle. This hurried sketch would eventually become the VW Panel Van, and it is easy to see why its shape earned the vehicle the nickname, in some countries, of 'the bread loaf'. That sheet of paper still exists, and the iconic vehicle that resulted from that quick doodle, and which would go on to be used as van, pickup, ambulance, fire engine, school bus and camper, across the globe from Rotterdam to Rio, from Salford to Sydney, was little different from Ben Pon's original, rough jotting.

It was a brilliant concept – a VW chassis with a box over it instead of a saloon body, the driver sat over the front axle, the engine over the back and enough space in between for a good load. Pon presented the idea to Hirst, who immediately saw that this could be something that would answer a basic, Europe-wide need for a simple, reliable load carrier. Together they took the sketch to Hirst's superior officer, Colonel Radclyffe. Radclyffe was based at Minden and was, by all accounts, an intelligent and approachable man, but reluctantly he refused to sanction the vehicle's development and manufacture. The factory was already working flat out making Beetles, and he felt that setting up a new production line would be too disruptive. Added to that, the suppliers of key components for the Beetle, such as Bosch, SWF and Solex, were already overstretched and would be unable, in Radclyffe's opinion, to meet any further demands. Hirst was disappointed but didn't give up. He was canny enough to bide his time, and knew that eventually he would find a way to get Pon's idea into production.

It was a year later that the third key figure in the Camper Van saga, Heinrich Nordhoff, came into the story. Nordhoff was a former director general of the pre-war Opel-Werke factory in Brandenburg. At that time the largest truck manufacturing plant in Europe, the factory had been turning out 4,000 trucks a month, so Nordhoff was no stranger to the management of a large motor works. A university-trained mechanical engineer, Nordhoff was not a Nazi but a devout Catholic, and what would probably now be termed a 'workaholic'. While working as service department head at Opel he had been known to work a seven-day week and even to spend his holidays on the factory assembly lines. It was while working at Opel that he had been sent to America to study production and sales techniques in Detroit, the heart of the American car industry. He came home to

Germany well versed in production and marketing, and with a spirit and determination that drove him forcibly and relentlessly up the company ladder. By 1936 he was on the board of management at Opel, and by 1942 he was director general.

Though never a party member, Nordhoff had been given an award by the Nazis for his work turning out trucks, and was thus tainted by association. When Germany collapsed, Nordhoff was barred from senior management posts. To keep his family fed and clothed, he took a job repairing cars and vans in a backstreet Hamburg garage. Hirst, who was keen to see the VW works back in German hands, had heard about Nordhoff from a friend, and managed to track him down and invited him for an interview for a job as assistant manager. The interview went on for two days. Early on, Hirst realised the potential of the man and decided not to give him a middle-management job but to make him managing director of the whole factory. With typical North Country humour and a completely straight face, Hirst told Nordhoff that he was sorry but he couldn't recommend him for the job he had come for, that of assistant manager. Nordhoff immediately stood up and began to pack his briefcase, at which point Hirst told him that this was because he was going to make him director general. What Nordhoff thought of Hirst's little joke has not been recorded – not a lot, I expect.

Nordhoff immediately set about turning the plant into a highly efficient motor works. For six months he slept in a camp bed in his office and ate, slept and dreamed Volkswagen, becoming totally committed to the marque. The general opinion is that the two men didn't get on particularly well together. Hirst, it is said, disliked Nordhoff's stern and autocratic management style, but was pragmatist enough to know that liking Nordhoff was not part of the job description; both men had their jobs to do and, as long as they kept each other at arm's length, things would be fine. There seems to be some truth in this because, in later years, both men would go on to make statements that seem to indicate that there was little love lost between them. Nordhoff played down Hirst's part in the VW success story while Hirst, somewhat tongue in cheek, rubbed a bit of the glitter off Nordhoff's crown.

In 1954 in Zurich, Nordhoff declared in a speech:

On January 1st 1948, six months before the currency reform I took on the management of the Volkswagen Works. I was faced with a desolate heap of rubble, a horde of desperate people, the torso of a deserted town – an amorphous mass which had never had any organising principle, no factory organisation in a real sense, without a programme or any rational work organisation. So something new had to be created because there was nothing there and had never been anything to build on at all.

How Nordhoff could assert this when in 1946 alone Hirst had produced 10,000 cars in a bombed-out factory is certainly beyond my ken. Hirst himself, when asked how Nordhoff had managed to achieve his miracle, replied:

> Yes, that is as it is seen by the world perhaps. I think you could have put anybody in there, even a monkey, and it would have been a success. There was a huge factory, a labour force, a building, a good management already in place, a car that would sell, huge demand all over the world for light cars, and it could not fail even if you put the biggest fool in charge, it would have worked. I say anybody but I mean anybody with management skills and entrepreneurial sense.

I detect a slight whiff of powder in Hirst's statement and I reckon that, for once, Nordhoff might have pushed 'the English officer' a little too far. However, whatever he felt at the time about Nordhoff's autocratic manner, Hirst quietly got on with the job of getting on with the man. It was this wise decision, together with Hirst's own love of the Beetle and his respect for the German people which transformed the fortunes not just of VW but of Germany. The German people took a justified pride in the success of the VW factory, and began to see it as a symbol of the new Germany that was rising up out of the grey postwar years and the ruins of their country. Under Nordhoff's command Volkswagen eventually became the world's third-largest manufacturer of motor cars. It is no exaggeration to say that the fortunes of VW in those early years reflected what was happening to the whole German nation. By 1948 Nordhoff had the factory turning out 6,000 cars a year, weather depending (there were still chunks of the roof and windows missing). Hirst was soon to leave VW but, before he went, and knowing that if Nordhoff liked the idea he would go with it wholeheartedly, he put Pon's drawing in his hands. He couldn't have made a wiser or more important move.

'We had to build it by hook or crook,' he would later say. 'It was simply that Ben Pon was right; tradespeople needed transport for carrying tools and equipment.' Nordhoff immediately saw the immense potential of the light van, ordered a prototype to be made and gave the design department six weeks to come up with something. On 20 November 1948, the blueprints for what would eventually become the VW Type 2 arrived on his desk. The drawings showed a simple, load-carrying box van with the engine at the rear and the driver and passengers at the front sitting over the wheels, not at all dissimilar from Pon's original sketch. What made the van extremely effective as a commercial vehicle was the large load-carrying space thus created between the flat four, rear-mounted engine and the forward-placed seats. It made use of all the high-quality engineering that had gone into the Beetle and, in many ways, was simply a Beetle with a box slung over it. Nordhoff, in fact, stipulated that as many Beetle parts as possible be used in the new vehicle's construction.

A prototype was made, and testing began on 9 March 1949. Hirst would later recall how the first prototype was taken out for testing at night, for secrecy, and returned in the morning six inches lower – under a full load the floor had buckled and collapsed. Nordhoff ordered a modification, and the designers produced an innovative solution: two linear girders with five transverse sections were welded under the floor pan, turning the van into a unitary box on wheels. This gave it more strength and rigidity and made it well able to take the strain of a three-quarter-ton payload. The lines of the vehicle were smoothed out in the university of Braunschweig's wind tunnel, making the van more aerodynamic even than the Beetle. After a few minor adjustments such as moving the location of the exterior petrol filler cap to inside the engine compartment to prevent theft of the fuel (it was still in short supply), the first model of the Type 2 was ready. By the spring of 1949 the prototype light van had completed a 12,000km circuit of the test track and had also been driven to the edge of destruction on the war-blasted roads and the rutted cart tracks and lanes of the countryside of Lower Saxony.

In the August of 1949 Hirst finally left Wolfsburg in Nordhoff's hands, having played a major part in turning the factory from rubble and ruin to being one of the foremost car plants in mainland Europe. Along the way he had overseen the production of two of the world's most remarkable vehicles: the VW Beetle and the VW Transporter. Few men have had such a major impact in peacetime, not just on the motoring world but on the lives of an entire nation – not bad for a lad from Lancashire. Hirst, characteristically modest, would always play down his part in the rise of VW in later years, but he did admit to being proud of leaving behind him a factory that was given back into German hands reborn, remade and hugely important in the life of the new nation. Some historians have tried to play down the part played by Ivan Hirst in the rebirth of Volkswagen but the company's own historian, Ralf Richter, author of the only biography of the major, said in a BBC Radio 4 interview in 2003 that there is absolutely no doubt that but for the work of Ivan Hirst there would have been no VW. Strangely there was no great job in industry waiting for Hirst when he left the army. He took a desk job with the OECD (Organisation for Economic Co-operation and Development) in Paris, after which he was unemployed for a while. He eventually retired to live out his life in a small village in the Pennines above Greater Manchester, not far from where he was born, and where he eventually died, aged 84, in 2000. The people of Wolfsburg did not forget him, and now there is a street in the town named after him and a plaque telling the world how much Major Ivan Hirst had meant to the survival of Volkswagen.

There is no doubt that Hirst's training as an engineer was a major reason for VW's survival, but there is also no doubt that his training as a REME officer played a huge part too. Two tenets of army engineering were Inspection and Spares. Every vehicle leaving a REME workshop was thoroughly inspected to make sure it was in top condition, and it was further understood that there was no point in having a fleet of lorries or cars or tanks if you didn't have the spare parts to service them. So no car left the VW plant without a detailed and thorough inspection and, ever since Major

Ivan Hirst's day, VW have always made sure that spares for their vehicles are plentiful and readily available. It had always been Ivan Hirst's ambition to hand back the VW plant to the German people as a going concern and he had more than achieved that. On 8 September 1949, shortly after Major Hirst headed for Britain, Colonel Charles Radclyffe signed Decree 202 which transferred ownership of the VW factory to the Federal Republic of Germany.

One of the first products of that new regime was the VW van which, after a few more modifications, was ready to go into production. The only problem was that, so far, the vehicle had no name. There were various suggestions. 'Atlas' was one and 'Bulli' (Bulldog) was another, but Heinrich Lanz, producer of the Lanz Bulldog farm tractor, soon snookered that idea. Finally Nordhoff decided to simply call it the 'VW Transporter'. Under this name, in November 1949, it was launched at the Geneva motor show. There was a huge interest in the new vehicle, many orders were taken and by March 1950 the first vans were rolling out of the factory.

Nordhoff told the world:

Like our Bug is a car without compromises, so will our Transporter be without compromises. This is why we did not start from an available chassis but from the cargo space. This is the clean, no compromise principle of our Transporter. With this van and only this van, the cargo space lies exactly between the axles. In the front sits the driver and, in the back is the same weight due to the engine and fuel tank. We would have put the engine in the front without hesitation if this had been a better solution. However the famous 'cab above the engine' gave such horrendous handling characteristics when loaded that we never even considered it.

And, in a wry moment of faint sarcasm, he added, 'You can tell by the trees in the British zone how well the army lorries, built with this principle, handle on wet roads when they are not loaded.' He was, of course, correct. The design of the vehicle put the engine, gearbox and drivetrain at the rear, the passengers up the front and the load in between. With this kind of weight distribution, loaded or empty the vehicle was inherently stable. Many people see Nordhoff as a humourless autocrat, yet there is ample evidence that the man, strict and completely driven though he may have been, was not without a sense of fun. Describing the side loading doors, one of the most distinctive and innovative features of the Type 2, to the motoring press he said, 'Loading from the side is natural and normal – who would think of getting into a limousine from the back?'

The Transporter began to roll out of the factory and, as output and sales rose (from 300 in March 1950 to 700 in June), it became obvious that the Type 2 was exactly the type of light transporter van that Europe had been waiting for.

Within months an export market had started, and Ben Pon, the man whose sketch had started the whole thing off, took delivery of chassis numbers 2017 to 2026 in Holland, and soon the first Transporters were heading out across the Atlantic to the USA and Brazil. The meeting of three remarkable men had brought a factory and ultimately a country back from ruin and had created a light goods transporter that would, in time, become one of the twentieth century's most loved vehicles.

Chapter 4

Rail Cars and Ice-Cream Vans

By 9 October 1954 the factory in Wolfsburg had turned out no fewer than 100,000 Transporters, which, with their windowless sides, were now being referred to as 'panel vans'. This was a triumph in many ways, because not only had VW pulled itself up out of the rubble, it had also proved the doom-merchants wrong – not just Sir William Rootes, but earlier detractors. In 1939 the technical editor of the British car magazine the *Motor*, with reverse prescience, had said of the Volkswagen Beetle, '. . . so far as the British market is concerned our manufacturers can sleep quietly in their beds.' He'd obviously bought his crystal ball from somebody he met in a pub, and it was probably the exact same crystal ball used by the man who prophesied that by the year 2000 we would all be travelling round with jet packs strapped to our backs and would be taking all our food in tablet form. The naysayers couldn't have been more wrong, of course. In the 1950s the British car industry, having spent the war years turning out military vehicles, was short of both money and ideas. Hanging on to both pre-war practices and pre-war labour relations, British motor manufacturing was stagnating while VW was quietly turning into a world-class business. By 1955, only ten years after VE Day, more than a million Volkswagen cars had been built, a third of them for export, and demand for the Type 2 Transporter Panel Van was rising year on year.

The appeal of the VW Type 2 lay in a number of things: its load carrying capacity (it could shift its own weight in goods); its power (its engine, though small, had a high torque and its transmission was highly effective); its reliability (all the parts were tried and tested, and being air-cooled didn't freeze up or boil over); its simplicity (the engine was straightforward to work on and easy to get at); and its design (the Type 2 was a futuristic-looking vehicle for its time). Added to this, the Panel Van had long blank sides crying out for the sign painter's brush – it was a blank slate on which almost anything could be written. Small businesses that were working hard to get established in the new

Europe saw the Type 2 as both a superb load carrier and as a really smart way of advertising their business. The van, as it came from the factory, was offered in two colours: duck-egg blue or primer. Within months, 70 per cent of sales were of primed vehicles only, and sign writers all over Western Europe were busy painting names and logos on the sides of the new vans. The VW museum at Wolfsburg has some stunning examples of early Transporters in various company liveries, and at any of the many VW fests and jams you will see lovingly cared-for Panel Vans promoting their small businesses, from chocolate makers to parfumiers and organisations as disparate as fire departments and lunatic asylums. There was nobody else in Europe making such a versatile and trustworthy workhorse, and sales reflected this.

But there was also, of course, a need within Europe for another kind of vehicle, one that could move people about, and not just goods. Once the bombed-out streets had been repaired there were trains and buses in most of the major cities, and these were the modes of transport used by the majority of people in the post-war years. Growing up in Manchester in those days I remember well how people, whether they were travelling for work or pleasure, either walked or got on a train, bus or bike; there were very few private vehicles about. The first car appeared in our street when

I was around ten years old. It was a second-hand Ford Prefect, the apple of my mate's dad's eye, and was lovingly washed and waxed every Saturday afternoon. In Germany, in fact all over Western Europe, it was the same story – private cars were still a rarity.

But trams and buses weren't always convenient; they didn't run all the time and they didn't go everywhere. Small groups of people often needed moving about – everything from businessmen travelling to meetings, to aircrews moving from the hotel to the terminal to their aircraft. What was needed was a compact people carrier. The designers at Wolfsburg weren't slow to realise that the Type 2 body could be adapted to carry people as well as goods, so they designed a variant of the Type 2, known as the Kombi. The Kombi (*Kombinationskraftwagen* – combination motor vehicle) was a Panel Van turned into a basic, stripped-down minibus with three windows on each side of the body section behind the cab. It had a bare metal interior, no headlining and, behind the driver's bench seat, had two rows of seats secured to the floor with wing nuts. Basic though it was, with a payload of eight passengers it was ideally suited for getting small groups about in a hurry. The added attraction, of course, was that, with the seats out, the Kombi, even with its windows, could still be used, like the Panel Van, as a simple load carrier. This combination of load and people carrier would eventually become the vehicle of choice for coachbuilders when they began turning the Type 2 into a Camper Van.

The Kleinbus (Microbus in the UK and Stationwagon in the USA) was the next development of the Type 2, and was a dedicated people carrier with fixed seating; it was a much more luxurious version of the Kombi. In fact, if you look at many of the illustrations VW were using in their advertising at the time you will notice that the Kleinbus features heavily. Bernd Reuters, the graphic artist responsible for much of VW's early advertising graphic work, produced stunning images of the Kleinbus (which was soon given the nickname 'Samba') showing it ferrying business types and airline crews around. The Microbus Deluxe, launched in June 1951, was a sleek, ultra-luxurious version of the Samba, with brightwork strips and domed chromed hubcaps, and aimed very much at the top end of the market. In Reuters' illustrations the Samba looks for all the world like something that has come directly out of a science fiction comic or the 1936 Alexander Korda film, *Things to Come*. Nowadays, concourse Microbuses Deluxe, preened and primped for the 'Show and Shine' sections of VW bus shows, gather crowds like jam gathers wasps, because the vehicle is still a design masterpiece. Not only was the Samba's exterior sleek and futuristic, its interior was made to the same first-class standard. All the bare interior metal below the waistline was covered by fibreboard, which in its turn was covered in vinyl. The dashboard had been enlarged, and the steering wheel, gear knob and window winders were now in Ivoroid (celluloid artificial ivory). There was plush headlining, the seats were much more luxurious, and there were fixed ashtrays. The Samba had four windows each side instead of the Kombi's three, and as well as a canvas roll-back roof, it had eight skylights along the roof edge – in all, the Samba had twenty-three windows. This made the Kleinbus de Luxe look even more like something that Buckminster Fuller would have created or that Dan Dare might have driven into the sunset.

The last model in the Type 2 stable, the Pickup, completed the family in August 1952 and sold well from the very beginning. Its manufacture had called for a fair bit of retooling: the roof had to be truncated to separate the cab from the rest of the body; the rear wheel and the petrol tank had to be relocated to make the flat bed; and a tool locker was designed to fit under the flat bed behind the cab. Just as the simple Panel Van had been a blank slate on which businesses could advertise themselves with pride to the world, so the Pickup was a vehicle capable of an enormous number of uses. It could be a simple load carrier trucking men and materials about; give it a hooped canvas roof and fit it out with shelving and it became a mobile shop; with the addition of a ladder turntable it became a cherry-picker or even a fire-fighting vehicle; and with the addition of the correct gauge of flanged wheels, it could also be turned into a rail-track maintenance vehicle. The German rail network used a number of such adapted Pickups for working on their rail system.

Together with the Panel Van, the Pickup (later offered also in Double Cab format) catered for almost every conceivable use. There were ambulances, mobile kitchens, outside-broadcast vans sprouting high telescopic aerials, refrigerator vans, hi-top vans for the garment industry which could carry racks of clothes uncreased, mobile workshops, mobile post offices, air-sea rescue vans, tip-up trucks – if you could imagine a use for a commercial vehicle, the VW Type 2 in one of its many forms could do it. There was even a dedicated iron lung carrier during the terrible days of the polio epidemic, and a number of Kombis were also converted into hearses. A four-wheel drive, all-terrain version of the van and one electric-powered prototype were also developed but neither model got into full production.

Nowadays specialised vehicles like the fire engines and ambulances are collectors' items and are zealously conserved, polished lovingly and shown off at the many

Dubfests and VW fairs that are held around the world. One of the highlights of a recent Camper Van festival I attended was a parade of original VW fire engines in full livery. To the crowd's delight they were raced around the field in the sunshine, lights flashing and sirens howling. These classic, iconic vehicles are no longer work buses but cherished, working, museum pieces, kept alive by enthusiasm and hard work and by the thousands of suppliers of spare parts scattered all over the globe that can find you anything from a tail light for a 1963 Samba to an oil seal for a 1972 Bay Window. Yet there is one model which is still doing the same job more than half a century later, though it was never made by Volkswagen and was only given official approval as a conversion after it had met their strict safety regulations: the Westfalia Kampervan – but that is a story for later pages of this book.

By the last months of 1954, Nordhoff had come to realise that demand for the Type 2 in all its many variations would soon be too much for the Wolfsburg works to deal with. More than 100,000 Type 2s had been made, and the waiting list for vehicles was rising daily. As well as building the Type 2 the works was of course still turning out the Type 1 Beetle by the hundreds of thousands, and the Beetle's incredible popularity across the world meant that output of that vehicle was increasing year on year, putting its own strains and demands on the VW works. One major problem was the lack of available manpower; 24,000 people (more than two thirds of the population of Wolfsburg) worked at VW, and without mass immigration there were no more workers to be had. Clearly, if VW were to continue as an expanding major company, something had to be done.

Hanover, 70 kilometres away, had a large and available skilled workforce, good communications and plenty of space for a new factory; and since there was every sign that the demand for the Type 2 was going to carry on increasing, Nordhoff decided to move the manufacture of the Type 2 there. Ground was broken for VW Hanover on 1 March 1954 and, as a perfect illustration of the amazing rebirth of Germany, the first Type 2 to be made there, a Pickup finished in the standard dove blue, came off the line two years almost to the day on 8 March 1956 – an amazing feat even by the standards of today. By the time a further three years had passed no fewer than half a million Type 2s had been produced at the Hanover works.

In the world of motor manufacturing, like the world of fashion, innovation and change are major driving forces. Competition is immense and new designs are hush-hush, kept under wraps until finally being launched in front of the motoring press to gasps of astonishment and the blitz of camera flash guns at the world's motor shows. Yet, from its first conception in 1950 until its demise in the late 1960s the Type 2 Splitty changed very little – on the surface at least. Much of this was down to the iron grip that Nordhoff had on VW. He was a practical man and very much the traditionalist; innovation and change for their own sakes were something beyond his ken. If his 'box on wheels' did what was needed, then why change it? By the time the Splitty had ceased production in 1967, just before the works shut down for their August break, the last one rolling off the assembly line was little different from the very first van that had rolled out at Wolfsburg seventeen years earlier.

This was due, I believe, not simply to Nordhoff's stubbornness, but to the fact that the vehicle was so well designed and well supported from its very beginnings that there was little real need to change things.

The van was incredibly reliable, and if it did, by any chance, need something doing to it, there was an excellent VW dealer network worldwide with highly trained mechanics and easy access to spare parts. In fact the Type 2 and the Beetle had so many parts in common that your Camper Van could be repaired almost anywhere in the world (with the exception perhaps of both polar ice caps). Since both the Beetle and Type 2 penetrated into some of the more remote corners of the planet, it followed that a breakdown in Ulan Bator was not the kind of disaster it might be for a Land Rover, and many of the adventurers' tales that feature the Type 2 talk about major repairs being carried out in the back-street workshops of places like Thailand and Colombia.

The van could carry its own weight in goods and people, and had amazing traction both on and off the road because of the rear engine's position above the back wheels. Since it was air-cooled, it had no water to freeze or boil over and no radiator to get holes in or rubber water hoses to perish. It started first time in any kind of weather and could be driven to extreme limits without breaking down. The Type 2 was also economical, something that motoring press reviewers of the time often praised; fuel consumption on the 1200 engine, for example, ran at an average 24 to 29 mpg while a similar van coming out of Detroit would have guzzled up twice that amount.

The downside of this, from a fashionista's point of view, was that VW, and Nordhoff in particular, saw little need for major changes in the Camper Van's overall image. While this made for a great deal of brand loyalty amongst Type 2 lovers, it also meant that changes were slow in coming and were never revolutionary. It took ten years, for example, for VW to fit a fuel gauge to the Panel Van. Nordhoff considered such things as frippery and a sign of decadence; instead, the Panel Van had a reserve tank and a tap to let the reserve fuel into the main system.

As Nordhoff said in an address he gave to the American Association of Automotive Engineers in 1958:

> I see no sense in starting anew every few years with the same teething troubles, making obsolete all the past. I went out on a limb. Offering people an honest value, a product of highest quality, with low original cost and incomparable resale value appealed to me more than being driven round by a bunch of hysterical stylists trying to sell people something they don't really want to have. And it still does . . . Every single part of this car has been improved over the years – these will continue to be our model changes.

Yet, though to us lesser motoring mortals the differences seem minimal, as Nordhoff stated, there were, in fact, a great many subtle modifications over the years, and the trained eyes of Camperfanatics can tell, at the drop of a filler cap, the difference between a 1954 Panel Van and a 1957 Panel Van.

As Europe began to grow more prosperous, people started to want more from life. House furnishings and clothes moved away from the plain utilitarian styles of the war years and began to reflect the spirit of hope that was infusing the new Europe. In like manner, people began to ask more of their cars and vans. The Type 2's body underwent a number of modifications. Quite early in its life a short prow was built over the van's windscreen, housing vents that would let air into the vehicle for cooling. The large barn door of the engine compartment was made much smaller and a tailgate built above it – this gave access to the rear of the load space and meant that, in the Samba for example, passengers' luggage could be stowed more easily. There were other modifications to such things as driving mirrors, trafficators and headlamps. These changes were made to bring the van into line with some of the new safety regulations being enforced in both Europe and America (America, for example, insisted on over-riders being fitted to the front bumpers of the vehicle). But these were small bodywork changes, and, to the non-cognoscenti, there is to all intents and purposes no major structural or design difference between an early Splitty and the Splitty as she was in the last year of her manufacture.

The engine, though, did change very considerably over those years. At 1131cc the original Type 2 flat four was fine for 1950 but within a handful of years began to seem seriously underpowered. Various tweaks with cylinder bore size and the carburettor had given the engine a little more horsepower but, compared to some of the new light commercial vehicles that were coming out of Detroit, the van definitely seemed lacking in oomph. This was rectified when the engine capacity was upped in 1953 to 1192cc. An increase of only 59cc might not seem a giant step but it took the vehicle from 25 horsepower to 30, and its top speed to from 50mph to 60mph. VW actually put a sticker on the dashboard warning drivers not to go faster than 50mph but most drivers ignored it, and there are many stories of drivers of performance vehicles on German autobahns being overtaken by Type 2s being driven flat out.

And there, at a quoted 1200cc, the engine more or less stayed until the sixties came along. Slight modifications were made to give it a little more vroom but even though things like boring out the valve seats and installing better carburetion gave the engine a slightly better performance it still wasn't enough, and it was 1963 before any major change in the Type 2 engine came about.

At 1500cc the new engine, launched in January of that year, gave the van a maximum speed in excess of 75mph (though VW, perhaps for safety reasons, claimed it was 10mph less). Nordhoff was so worried about accident claims that he had a governor fitted to the carburettor to limit the engine's power. Many drivers, alarmed at putting their foot down to overtake a slow-moving wagon, and suddenly finding that the floor had turned to rubber, simply did the obvious: took a spanner and whipped the governor off.

As the engine changed year by year, so too did the transmission – from a fairly clunky 'crash' gearbox to full synchro. The early gearbox and transmission were fine for their time but were typical of the 1950s. Synchromesh, which enables us modern manual-shift drivers to slip effortlessly up and down the gears, was not common in those days, and drivers had to learn to 'double de-clutch' in order to shift between gears. This wasn't a difficult procedure but it did mean that you had to know your engine and listen attentively to the revs. Once you judged the time was right you dipped the clutch, slipped the gears into neutral, let the clutch out for a second, dipped it again, slipped it into the gear you wanted, then let the clutch out a last time. It sounds much harder than it is, but it did call for some understanding and appreciation of engine speed. This meant that people who were engine tone-deaf often amused small boys by roaring, juddering and crunching their way through the gearbox at traffic lights, driving their cars away leaping and lurching like drunken robots (the 1950s term for such a getaway was 'Kangaroo petrol'). By 1959 synchromesh had been fitted to all four forward gears.

The brakes, right until the demise of the Splitty, were still the drum type; though, to be fair, they were reported as stopping the vehicle firmly and having no discernible fade. Still, when the van was fully loaded, the driver had to drive constantly with the knowledge that stopping was not an 'on-a-sixpence' affair. Disc brakes would not come on the scene until the arrival of the Bay Window model.

The six-volt system was another problem. As some-one who spent many a night peering ahead into the murk and fog of the North Country, trying to see what was road and what was boggy moor or potato field, I can tell you that its lighting system was not the Type 2's best selling point. Surprisingly the Type 2 got its new twelve-volt system a whole year before the Beetle, and it was a modification eagerly awaited and much appreci-ated. Though I never noticed it myself, there were some parts of Europe and the Americas where a particularly cold spell could produce a severe voltage drop in the small six-volt Bosch batteries; the engine would be ready to go but the starter would fail to turn over. Not the nicest thing to discover on an icy morning when you're trying to get to work or get the kids to school. The new twelve-volt system meant that the engine always started, no matter how cold, and also meant that night driving was no longer a slow and terrifying experience. Yorkshire sheep, for example, would no longer suddenly appear out of the night on Saddleworth Moor like woolly phantoms illuminated only by two jam jars worth of very weak fireflies. For some time it had been possible to have your Type 2 converted to a twelve-volt system, but this fairly expensive extra was now standard. Today many early models of the Type 2 have been brought up to spec, and though this might mean that they are no longer 'stock', as aficionados of the originals call them, your van is a much safer and more comfortable ride – trust me. My old friend the Irish folksinger Christy Moore spent his apprenticeship travelling round the English folk clubs in a six-volt Beetle in the early sixties. As he once pointed out to me, like our early rock 'n' roll bus it was not a great ride at night – every time you plugged in the cigarette lighter the headlights went out.

Chapter 5

Overland to Kangaroo Valley

BY THE TIME THE LAST Splitty made its way out of the Hanover works in 1967 the van was not only known across the world but was being made, or at least assembled, in several other countries.

South Africa imported its first Beetles and Transporters through a company called SAMAD (South African Motor Assemblers and Distributors) in 1951, and in August that year the first Beetle, assembled from a CKD (Complete Knock Down) kit, came out of their Uitenhage factory. Everything: engine, panels, seats, gearbox – even the ashtrays – was made and crated in Germany, then shipped by sea to be assembled in South Africa. In 1952 SAMAD (while still importing fully assembled Beetles and Transporters) increased the assembly of Type 2s from CKD kits imported from Hanover as the vehicles began to garner interest throughout South Africa. Over the next few years there was a gradual changeover in the SAMAD works from CKD to fully pressed and machined vehicles as assembly lines were built in the factory, and as many parts as possible were sourced locally. In 1956, sensing a growing market and realising that this could be a foothold into the southern part of the continent, VW bought a controlling share of the company, and by 1966 the company became Volkswagen of South Africa.

In a country like South Africa where wildlife and natural wonders are on the doorstep, the Camper Van presented a wonderful opportunity for people to get out into the wilderness. As well as CKD Transporters, CKD Westfalia Kampmobile interiors were likewise sent over in kit form to be fitted into the Type 2s in Uitenhage. When the Bay Window model came along, VW of SA began production of its own model, the Kampmobile, which used Westfalia parts or copies of them. After 1967, when construction of the Splitty ended in Europe, South Africa continued to make Type 2 vans, though by then they were mostly constructed from Brazilian parts.

Australia was another big market for VW. The first Type 2s arrived there in 1953 – a mixture of CKD and fully assembled models – but it was 1955 before the Australian CKD Type 2 really became established. That year, 546 were assembled in a factory in Melbourne and 2,989 the year after. The Type 2's popularity was enhanced when Australian government agencies such as the army, the air force and the post office ordered fleets of vans (the post office alone ordered 1,200). As in South Africa, production gradually changed from CKD to full manufacture, and engine shops and pressing plants eventually produced a vehicle that was 40 per cent Australian sourced. In 1964 VW (as in South Africa) bought out the Australian assemblers and founded Volkswagen Australia.

Over the years modifications were made to the Ozzie Type 2 to enable it to deal better with the Australian climate. In particular, the air-intake vents were moved from below the van's waistline to above, and were lengthened to get more air around the engine, helping it to cope with Oz's non-Germanic weather system and the grit and dust of the outback roads. Australian versions of the van were more often than not fitted with 'roo bars' to ward off jaywalking kangaroos, something the average citizen driver of Glasgow or Guttenberg would not have been troubled with.

Incidentally the drier climate in Australia has meant that Oz Vee Dubs have suffered hardly at all from the ravages of the weather, and second-hand, rust-free, right-hand drive models have been shipping to the UK for years. In the 1960s and '70s they were often driven overland all the way from Australia by Ozzies heading for 'Kangaroo Valley' (as London's Earls Court was then known). Once in Blighty they were often parked up and sold outside Australia House and would sometimes find themselves being driven back along the self-same overland route they had arrived by, returning through Europe and Asia, driven overland by another bunch of hippies – this time Pom hippies heading south. The Oz trade has continued to this day, and there are several UK-based firms bringing in rust-free RHD (right-hand drive) Oz vans. In fact the complaint often heard expressed in Australia today is that, 'The Poms are nicking all our bloody Kampers.'

It has to be said that, important as these outpost productions were, compared to the output from Hanover, the Southern Hemisphere production, though not to be sneezed at, was not a major part of VW's output. To give an example: in 1964 the total world production of vehicles was in excess of 200,000, of which less than 7 per cent were made outside Germany.

But when you look at the production figures over the entire life of the Type 2, one country stands out above all others: Brazil. Brazil's links with VW go back to

1950 when José Thompson who was head of a major car-importing firm based in São Paulo, began importing the first Beetles into South America. Imports at first were small in number but when, in 1953, Volkswagen do Brasil SA was established, with Hanover owning 80 per cent of the firm and Brazilian shareholders the remaining 20 per cent, things began to change. At first CKD units were assembled in São Paulo, but in 1957 a new factory was opened on the main highway between the city and the sea, and by the end of 1960 half a million had been manufactured in Brazil. Many Brazilian vans are still working as buses and as trucks in the countries of South America. Easily repaired and simple to maintain, they chug along still, more than fifty years after they were made.

From the earliest years of VW's postwar life, the USA was a very important market for VW. Compared to the larger US gas-guzzling vans and pickups, both the Beetle and the Transporter looked quite small and underpowered, but they were economical to run, were safe, quirky vehicles and they captured a niche market. They weren't the kind of vehicles that Good Old Boys would chug along in, slugging beer, singing along to Country music with the gun rack in the back – not too many rednecks drive Camper Vans, in my experience. But both the Beetle and the Type 2 had their aficionados who were intensely loyal to the brand, and of course it was in America that the Camper Van first achieved its totemic status as an icon of Liberty and the Alternative Society. However there were one or two hiccups: US safety regulations often called for modifications to the model, especially the type of bumper bars that would be allowed and the position of lights (the old semaphore trafficators were replaced by 'bullet'-style indicators in 1955, for example). And then, of course, there was the world-famous 'Chicken War'. 'Ah, the Chicken War,' I hear you murmur. 'We were wondering when he would get round to that.'

Well, during the early 1960s, France and West Germany placed tariffs on imports of US chicken which were heavily subsidised and which, at that time, were flooding into the continent at the expense of home producers, throwing many small- and medium-sized chicken farmers out of business. In a tit-for-tat move, in January 1964, President Johnson imposed a 25 per cent tax (almost ten times the average US tariff) on potato starch, dextrin, brandy and light trucks.

In fact, when the documents relating to the Chicken War were released years later, it turned out that the war was nothing remotely to do with chickens at all and was a quid pro quo negotiated between President Johnson and the United Auto Workers' president

Walter Reuther. Reuther, who was deeply resentful of the inroads European car manufacturers had been making into the USA, had planned to initiate a strike just prior to the 1964 election, and to get him to call off the industrial action Johnson, worried (as are all politicians) that he would lose votes, agreed to curtail Volkswagen's shipments to the United States.

The 'Chicken Tax', as it came to be known, had an immediate effect on the import of German-built Type 2s, and figures show that sales to the US dropped by about a third. By 1971 imports of Volkswagen cargo vans and pickup trucks – which were the main reason for a tax which had nothing to do with chickens – had fallen to close on zero. Nowadays, post-1971 Type 2 vans and pickups can be seen in the USA, but they are exceedingly rare. By the way, just as a point of interest, it seems that at the time of writing the Chicken Tax has not in fact been repealed, and still remains in effect.

By the mid-sixties the Type 2 could be found in pretty much every country in the world. Outwardly little had changed, though power units and braking had been much improved. Where other car manufacturers produced a new vehicle every August, VW (or more accurately Heinrich Nordhoff) seemed content to trim a little here and add a little there. Many writers have condemned Nordhoff for his conservatism and his autocratic nature, and have claimed that he held VW back with his entrenched attitude. Eventually of course the Japanese motor industry made massive incursions into the market both in Europe and in the USA, and sales of the Beetle and the Type 2 fell considerably. But this was nothing to do with lack of innovation and had everything to do with money; US car makers constantly introduced new models, as did French and Italian manufacturers, but Japan, with its lower labour costs and its amazing ability to produce quality vehicles far cheaper than the US or Europe, soon impacted on both markets.

As the mid-sixties came along even Nordhoff realised that some major changes needed to be made to the Type 2 and, in 1964, work began on designing a successor to the Splitty. In fact, although many of Nordhoff's critics have accused him of intransigence and of being far too conservative, it was he who brought in the design engineers from Porsche who were to work on the new VW van. The one stipulation Nordhoff made was that all models from the Panel Van to the Pickup had to be ready for launch by 1967. In the end all but one were finished and complete.

By the end of its manufacturing life in 1967, the Splitty had come to be known and loved across the globe, and close on two million vehicles had rolled off the lines in Germany, Brazil, South Africa and Australia

– in fact Splitty production continued in Brazil until 1975 where a further 400,000 were made. In the last year of its life in Europe, the Splitty accounted for 15 per cent of all Volkswagen sales, which isn't bad for something that started life looking like a rough sketch of a pan loaf in a Dutchman's notebook. But for the Splitty in Europe, 1967 was the end of the line. This, the simple VW Transporter, was the van I misspent my youth in, playing rock 'n' roll around the dance halls, nightclubs, pubs, working men's clubs and other dives of northern England – a simple Panel Van, sealing-wax red, basic and yet completely reliable.

The new model launched in 1967, was given the title Type 2:2 – Nordhoff, it has to be said, was not tremendously creative when it came to naming his vehicles. The new Transporter had more or less the same footprint as the Splitty – it was only five inches longer – and it still had its engine at the rear, but in many other aspects it was a very different animal. The windscreen now was a single unit with wraparound sides which made for much greater visibility and gave the vehicle its nickname, 'The Bay Window'. The dashboard was no longer made from pressed steel but was a more safety-conscious plastic affair, with the speedometer and petrol gauge sunk in to make them more readable. The double doors had been replaced by a single sliding door which meant that (in Britain and Australia at least) you no longer had to open hinged doors on the traffic side. The engine was now a healthy nominal 1.6 litres (actually 1584cc) which meant that the van could drive all day quite happily at 65mph, and drive quite pleasantly too because, with new linkage systems and axles, both road holding and handling were much improved. I can vouch for this personally, having driven both a 'stock' Splitty and my own Bay Window, Molly – she may be a slow old bus, but sitting high up above the road with a wide view of the scene ahead, a large wooden-rimmed steering wheel and more responsive steering, I find her a joy to drive.

In the first version of the Bay, braking was still via drums front and rear, though now a dual-circuit system meant that should one fail the other would take over. The van still had to be driven quite defensively (it still does) and you have to be aware that you are driving quite slowly and therefore holding up impatient drivers (particularly Homo Plaustrum Niveus – White Van Man). Not only that – if you do need to overtake something moving slower than you (a hedgehog for example), you have to plan quite far ahead; likewise with the braking. Molly, like all later Bay models, has front discs and rear drums, but it's always as well to leave a respectful distance between her and the vehicle in front.

The new Transporter was an immediate success and, unlike the Splitty, where models such as the Pickup had been introduced piecemeal after the original Panel Van, all the various types of Bay Window (except the Double Cab Pickup) were launched simultaneously: Panel Van, Kombi, Microbus and Pickup. The Bay Window was a great success from the day of its launch. Even the most stuck-in-the-mud Splitty fans gave it a grudging thumbs up, and the motoring press at large was almost ecstatic.

> The VW bus stands in a class of its own. It's such a practical shape for carrying people and their recreational accoutrement that, unfortunately the tendency is to cram more into it than its engine will handle. In the two weeks we lived with it, the bus did its job which was to take us wherever we wanted to go. The fact that it required twenty more minutes to make the run from Los Angeles to San Diego seemed quite unimportant when, the next day, we purchased the family Christmas tree and carried all seven feet of it, branches unbroken, with the top protruding through the sunroof. You can't do that in a Cadillac, despite its 375 horsepower.

In keeping with the VW philosophy, inherited from Nordhoff, of only changing things when necessary, the Bay's design altered little during its lifetime. Real Camper Van experts can tell from looking at a van's tail light cluster exactly where it was made – and probably the date the bumper was fitted and the name of the girlfriend of the bloke who tightened the nuts on the wheel. My interest, while keen, is more general. There is one trick, however, that we amateur Camper Van fans can employ to impress our friends: you can date a Bay to before or after 1973 by the position of the front indicator lights. Pre-1973 they are below the headlamps just above the bumper; after that year they appear above the headlamps on either side of the front grille. With that knowledge you will be able to win pints, prizes and admiration wherever you go. By 1975 new, safer, bumpers had been fitted and, for no reason that anybody has ever been able to explain, the VW roundel on the front was made much smaller. Non-visible safety advances included a collapsible steering column and a crumple zone.

The Bay had a shorter life than the Splitty (in Europe at least – they are still being made in Brazil) but in that shorter life it sold more models worldwide, and you are more likely to see an old Bay on the road on its way to the coast or the hills than an old Splitty. By the time they stopped manufacturing Bays in Germany in July 1979, VW had sold more than 2.4 million. The

remarkable thing is not that the Bay became less popular with the motoring public, it seems that VW simply
ran out of ideas. There was a worldwide rise in the number of four-wheel drive vehicles being manufactured,
particularly in Japan. But because of internal company
politics, VW (though it made prototypes) never added
a 4x4 Transporter to its stable. Porsche engineers who
worked closely with VW had produced designs for such
a model but their ideas had been ignored. There was
perhaps a small element of complacency at work here
because having the rear engine over the back axle did
give the vehicle amazing traction and meant that on
some hill climbs it actually out-performed comparable
Japanese 4x4s. But a four-wheel drive version of the
Bay, particularly when converted into a Camper Van,
would surely have been a great seller. Can you imagine
travelling the Australian bush or the African safari parks
in an all-terrain Camper Van? One Australian motoring journalist wrote, 'If they made a 4x4 version, there
would be a queue from Sydney to Melbourne.' Internal
politics, or perhaps a momentary lapse in joined-up
thinking meant that there would never be a queue
crossing Western Australia, and as sales of the Bay began
to falter, the designers at VW went back to the drawing
board and produced yet another version of 'the box on
wheels'.

The third generation of Transporter, the Type 2 T3 (also confusingly called the T25 and Caravelle), was nicknamed the Wedge in Britain because of its shape, and was known as the Vanagon in the USA. It was to be the last of the German air-cooled, rear-engined buses. It was bigger and heavier and more aerodynamic than its predecessors, and its wedge front is pleasing to some – but in your writer's humble opinion the Type 3 and the models that have followed, the T4 and T5, lack the classic lines of the Splitty and the Bay. The Wedge did exactly what it said on the packet: it was a powerful box on wheels that could carry stuff economically and was another superb example of German engineering. But, to my eyes, it lacks the kindlier, more human face that the Bay, and the Splitty in particular, showed to the world. As Laurence Meredith writes in his excellent book on the Transporter, the Wedge's face was 'no longer happy or smiling; it had taken on a lean and hungry look, reflecting Western political and social life of the time'.

The Wedge was wider and longer and the internal space had been increased still further by lowering the engine compartment. The range, as before, was made up of Panel Van, High Top Panel Van, Single and Double Cab Pickup, Kombi and Microbus. Again the vehicle had an immediate and mostly positive welcome from the motoring press, though some did lament the loss of the rounded, friendly curves. The Wedge soldiered on with an air-cooled engine for three years until 1982, when the engine was replaced by a 1.6 litre diesel or 1.9 litre water-cooled flat four. The diesel proved particularly popular because it ran so economically; at 38 mpg it made a big impact in the USA as an economical load carrier, and when converted to a Camper Van it made holidays a much cheaper affair. A great number of converted Wedge campers can still be seen on the roads and even (as a class of their own) at some VW festivals. In 1989 Volkswagen produced yet another Transporter model, the Type 4. This was shaped quite differently to the Wedge – it was smoother, more rounded and, in a drastic break from the past, had the engine mounted at the front. For many VW aficionados this was the bale of hay that discomfited the camel to its mortal end and, to their way of thinking, the glory days of the VW Camper Van were over.

Which in one way is true, though VW continued, and still continue to make great vans. In fact the camping conversion of their latest model, the T5, is the first conversion to be made completely by VW, and is a truly luxurious short-wheel based Camper Van. Like its great-granddaddy the Splitty, it will go anywhere, is a great camping vehicle and, unlike many of the bigger mobile homes you see thundering up the motorways today, it can still be parked in a normal saloon space.

There are rumours that, just as they made a world-class retro version of the Beetle, VW are set fair to make a retro version of the Splitty, but I must stress that, so far at least, this seems to be just a rumour. Pictures of just such a prototype have been seen, but nothing more. If it were to be anything like the new Beetle it would be another world-class vehicle from VW. We have one of the new Beetles in the family and she is loved to bits. If they needed a designer for the new granddaughter of the Splitty, made in the same futuristic mode, perhaps VW ought to go to Holland and find somebody with a Dutch general's uniform, a spiral-bound notebook, a big cigar and a lot of common sense.

Chapter 6

The Camper Van – From Work Bus to Tin Tent on Wheels

SAY THE WORDS 'CAMPER VAN' and the majority of people naturally think of the Vee Dub, rather than, say, the Commer Highwayman, the Bedford Dormobile or the Citroën Nomad, so iconic have the Splitty and the Bay become. Yet the camper van (or even Kampervan) as such wasn't invented by Volkswagen; far from it, cars and trucks, modified and turned into mobile holiday homes, have been with us since the earliest years of the motor car. In fact, when you think about it logically, the motor home is nothing more than the natural descendant of the horse-drawn caravan. Just as cars and lorries replaced carriages and carts, so the motor-drawn caravan, and later the motor home, where the traction unit and living quarters were all one, took the place of the old horse-drawn gypsy vardo and the steam-engine-drawn showman's van. It seems that, as ever, it was America that led the way in the conversion of cars and lorries into motor homes, and this is hardly surprising since it was America, and Henry Ford in particular, that first began the mass production of motor cars.

However, it was not just the greater availability of vehicles in the USA that inspired people to convert them into mobile homes. Many social historians believe that the inspiration came from a fundamental instinct that is hard-wired into the American psyche. The notion of Manifest Destiny, whereby the Almighty had provided an open continent specifically for the white man's advancement, was the bedrock of the American Dream, the idea of the frontiersman pushing his way ever westward along the Oregon Trail was central to the way Americans saw themselves. There were a few problems encountered along the way, of course: snakes, grizzly bears, impassable deserts and several hundred thousand Native Americans who were not all that happy at being cleared off their newly 'discovered' land. But the hunger for land was fierce, and the snakes and bears were easily dealt with. As for the natives? Well, beyond a few major hiccups, like the battles of Little Big Horn and Wounded Knee, the Red Men were soon subdued and moved onto reservations out of the way, leaving the land opened up and there for the exploiting. Any 'pesky Injuns' that were still hanging around came in handy as part of a picturesque backdrop – Monument Valley on its own is good, but Monument Valley with a bunch of buckskin-clad natives in the middle distance is even better.

Once the West had been won by John Wayne and Hopalong Cassidy, it wasn't all that long – less than half a century, perhaps – before Henry Ford set about transforming, not just America, but the whole world with the motor car. Ford didn't invent the motor car, of course, but he did invent the assembly line, and it was mass production on this scale that brought about a revolution that would eventually mean that there are not many places left on our small, old planet that are not now accessible by car.

The new immigrants that flooded into America in the early years of the century mostly went to live in the great industrial cities that were spreading ever outwards and upwards. Increased mechanisation in agriculture also meant that there was less labour needed on the land. People moved from the country to the cities, and cities themselves spread and grew more populous. Once the motor car had become more readily available and new roads had been built to take them, long-distance travel soon became a part of everyday life and, to a nation like America that was constantly on the move, the notion of a motorised covered wagon or hut on wheels had great appeal.

As the cities grew and as the roads snaked out across the continent to join them together it began to dawn on some individuals that America was eating up its wild spaces faster than any country had ever done before. America, the fastest growing industrial nation, also became the first country in the world to recognise the need for the creation of national parks when, in 1872, Yellowstone was established as the world's first truly national park.

The driving force behind the new national parks was the Sierra Club, founded in San Francisco in 1892 by John Muir (1838–1914), an immigrant Scot and a truly remarkable man who did more to preserve the American wilderness than any other single individual. He wrote books, letters and essays and lobbied tirelessly and remorselessly for the unspoiled lands he loved. He saw the death of the wilderness as the death of something in man, and saw his mission, according to one biographer, as 'saving the American soul from total surrender to materialism'. He once wrote: 'Thousands of tired, nerve-shaken, over-civilised people are beginning to find out that going to the mountains is going home; that wilderness is a necessity; and that mountain parks and reservations are useful not only as fountains of timber and irrigating rivers, but as fountains of life.' The Sierra Club, composed of hardy men and women who thought nothing of tramping months through the mountains, is still one of the most potent forces for conservation on the planet (it has more than a million members). It has, as its stated mission, 'To explore, enjoy, and protect the wild places of the earth; To practice and promote the responsible use of the earth's ecosystems and resources; To educate and enlist humanity to protect and restore the quality of the natural and human environment; and to use all lawful means to carry out these objectives.'

Muir's writings, together with Mark Twain's *Roughing It* and Walden's *Thoreau* were to the American outdoors movement what Wordsworth and the Romantics were to the British, and those Americans who wanted to kick out against the new mass-consumer culture found some solace in these writers. It is a strange twist of irony that the people who wanted to get away from it all often used that new invention of mass consumerism, the motor car, to carry them away from the clamour and pollution of cities like New York, San Francisco and Chicago. They went out into the Great Lakes, the high country and the national parks, carrying their tents and billycans, dixies and bedrolls strapped to the running board or stashed in the boot. As the cities grew, so did the outdoors movement, and it soon became quite a business, with shops and mail order firms setting themselves up to kit out the 'autogypsies', as some were beginning to call them, and new magazines like *Outdoor Life* and *Motor Camper and Tourist* providing them with information.

Among the first 'autogypsies' were none other than Henry Ford himself and his friend, Thomas Edison, the inventor. They regularly went on long car-camping expeditions together around America's wild places, taking their families, friends and servants with them. They were soon joined by Harvey Firestone, the tyre manufacturer, and John Burroughs, the famous naturalist. The group became known as the Vagabonds, and Vagabondage became quite fashionable amongst the moneyed classes. For ten years, from 1914 to 1924, the Vagabonds travelled the roads. Newspapermen and photographers followed them everywhere, and their exploits filled the gossip columns, spreading the idea of autocamping even further.

Nobody knows who the first person was that went from auto-camping or sleeping rough in their car to building a rudimentary canvas or wooden hut-like superstructure onto the car's chassis, turning it, in effect, into the first Camper Van. Whoever it was, the

idea took hold and by the beginning of the twentieth century, rough ancestors of the Camper Van were
beginning to appear on America's roads. Early pictures
from before the First World War show timber-framed
superstructures chugging along the roads, some like
garden sheds on wheels, others more sophisticated with
Tudor-style leaded windows and back porches. Many
were built on Model T frames, but the most effective
were built on truck frames which took the extra weight
and the rougher roads quite happily. Soon professional
coachbuilders, taking notice of the increasing popularity of the handmade camper tops, began converting
vehicles into camper vans for sale, advertising their
'camp cars', as they came to be known, in new magazines like *Motor Camper and Tourist*.

The organisation, Tin Can Tourists of America,
devoted to all things to do with autocamping, was
formed in Tampa, Florida in 1919 and was perhaps the
world's first caravan club. Some of the organisation's
early members still travelled in horse-drawn, gypsy
caravans. Others had canvas tents strapped to the running boards of their cars, but a growing number had
begun to bolt DIY, Heath Robinson bodies onto truck
and car chassis. Campgrounds were established so the
autocamper could play at being a gypsy while still enjoying all the home comforts. Meets were organised and

were overseen by somebody called the Mayor of Easy Street (the main street in the camp). They even had their own membership badge – a tin can welded to the vehicle's radiator cap. The organisation, in a slightly different form, is still in existence today, proclaiming on its website, 'Tin Can Tourists is an all make and model vintage trailer and motor coach club. Our goal is to promote and preserve vintage trailers and motor coaches through gatherings and information exchange.' The DIY motor homes of those early years were as many and varied as their owners; some were merely mobile huts, others looked more like Spanish galleons or bijou cottages.

As time went on the homes on wheels that lined the sidewalks of Easy Street began to become more sophisticated as richer owners decided that their vans should contain not just the basics but all the conveniences and knick-knacks of a modern home. Coachbuilders were not slow in picking up on this, and by 1910 the Pierce Arrow Motor Company was offering a landau for sale with tooled leather seating, a wash basin, stove, cooker, toilet and water tank for a mere $8,250 (roughly $190,600 in today's money). Typical of the new range of manufactured camp cars was the Lamsteed Kampcar designed by Samuel Lambert of St Louis, Missouri, the man who invented Listerine mouthwash. His Camper Van superstructure was designed to be bolted onto an existing motor chassis and was in production from 1915 to 1933. It cost $535 ($12,400 today) when first launched, slept four and had a folding table, a stove and a water tank. Lambert claimed his Kampcar superstructure could be fitted on a Model T chassis in six hours, and advertising copy promoting the van proclaimed: 'Make this the kind of vacation you've always dreamed about – enjoy the splendor of Yellowstone, the majesty of the Grand Canyon, visit balmy Palm Beach or the great North Woods. Go anywhere you wish – at your own hotel, eating your own cooking at your own table – all in great comfort and at a price you can easily afford.'

By the 1930s, the camp cars had become much more sophisticated and, at the top end of the market, were attracting some extraordinary customers – even Mae West succumbed to the idea of a palace on wheels, though she never used hers for vagabondage (though I'm sure she could have made something out of the name). Paramount Studios managed to entice her away from vaudeville and onto their film set by providing the great dame of single entendre with a mobile luxury pied-à-terre built on a 1931 Chevrolet base. It had a cooker and icebox, a dining table and chairs, and even had a back porch with a rocking chair. Mae West used it for several years.

The American camper van movement carried on growing until the Second World War when the country, once it was on a war footing, got on with the business of building tanks and battleships and big aeroplanes which they left stuck in German factory roofs. However, once the war was over, and people began to look forward to something like a normal life, interest in the mobile home revived and hundreds of companies that had been turning out parts for the war effort began to produce luxury camper vans and caravans. Prominent among them were Airstream and Winnebago, and both firms have gone on to produce vans which are absolute classics of their kind. Since the 1950s the RV (recreation vehicle) movement in the USA has mushroomed until now there are hundreds of RV clubs. In the city of Elkheart, Indiana, is the world's biggest (it just had to be) RV Museum and Hall of Fame, a massive complex which also has a conference centre, library and campground. The mobile homes that cross the American continent now are a universe away from the old wooden shacks on a Model T chassis that began the movement; now they have gourmet fitted kitchens, hot tubs and home cinemas.

I spent some time travelling across the southern states in a slightly more modest rented Winnebago 'palace on wheels' a few years back and found the whole experience fascinating. I would follow other RVs into the campgrounds to discover that they were being driven by octogenarians wearing ten-gallon hats and buckskins, while their mobile mansions sported decals and bumper stickers declaring, 'Spending the kids' inheritance' and 'Too old to work, too young to die, cruising the highways, bye bye.' One late afternoon, after travelling miles of desert highways, I pulled off the road at Stovepipe Wells in the heart of Death Valley to see that the campground was advertising a 'Bluegrass and Old Timey Night' for that very evening. I parked up, hooked up, made myself some dinner, showered and changed and set off with my mandolin for the mess hall about 8.30 p.m. only to meet a horde of retirees heading in the opposite direction. They were looking forward to their Ovaltine and their beds; things finish early in American RV land. Still, I suppose it must be quite tiring spending the kids' inheritance.

A similar motor home movement to that in the USA also took hold in Europe, though, initially, on a much smaller scale. In the UK the impulse behind the camping and Camper Van movement was not the Wild West and the Oregon Trail but the works of writers like Richard Jeffries, W.H. Davies and George Borrow. George Henry Borrow, who was born in Norfolk in 1803, was a multilinguist who seemed to be able to absorb languages through his skin. He knew Latin and Greek and could speak German, Russian, Spanish, Portuguese and Irish fluently. He also learned Romany, the language of the Roma or Gypsy people, and wrote two books about his travels with the Gypsies, *Lavengro* and *Romany Rye*. The latter book in particular gave the world's first industrialised society a whiff of the great outdoors, the open road and a freewheeling life away from the stink and clamour of the cities. Most people in the Western Europe of the early twentieth century were familiar with the sight of gypsy caravans trundling along country roads, or showman's vans parked on the fringes of the great travelling fairs. The sight of these freewheeling wagons must have touched something in the collective mind of the people. Even now, when I see the showman's wagons pulled up at the county fairs I get the same old townie's twitch for the open road, well away from the taxman and the vatman and the forms and rules and regulations and nonsensical detritus that pollute our daily lives.

It wasn't just Toad of Toad Hall or the middle-class romantics that were inspired to dreams of freedom by the notion of a canary-yellow caravan and the endless road that lay beyond the doorstep. Millions of people were trapped in the industrial slums and the great factories and forges that had transformed England from a 'green and pleasant land' into the world's workshop. Just a few steps away from the daily grind was the beckoning open road, and the country it led to exerted a magnetic pull on the workers' souls.

It has to be remembered that in historical terms, in Britain (and this is true of places like Germany too), the move from countryside to town had been a fairly recent phenomenon. The people who worked in the new mills and factories were only one generation away from the land, and the folk memories of many industrial workers went back deep into the fells and moors, the rivers and fields of an older, less damaged Britain. One of my favourite folk ballads, 'July Wakes', tells of two Lancashire cotton mill lads who spend their 'wakes' (holiday) week rambling and sleeping under the stars on and around Pendle Hill, the great witches' mountain that stands alone above the Ribble Valley. The final two verses of the song read:

Days carefree 'til Jack downcast
Watching larks and linnets racing past
Hears the hooters moan through the linnet's blast
To hell wit' looms

For Monday'll see us back in t'shed
Watching shuttles spewin' out miles and miles of thread

And we'll be weavin' fifty-one weeks of bread
And just one of life.

In the industrial cities of Britain and Ireland cycling clubs, rambling and walking clubs, climbing and mountaineering clubs were all created by people who sensed that real life lay not at the lathe, the work bench or the office desk but somewhere 'out there' where the larks and linnets sang, where the wind blew clean and the rivers and streams were not full of industrial filth. The outdoors movement that emerged as a result of the industrialisation of Britain was a broad church that embraced ramblers, cyclists and campers, and it was not long before motor campers were added to the list.

Chapter 7

An Englishman's Home is His VW Dormobile

RECORDS INDICATE THAT THE FIRST commercial camper van in Britain may well have been built in 1906 in Manchester by the Belsize Motor Co. It was far removed from the compact VWs that grace the roads nowadays, and was more like a showman's van than anything else. Almost 22ft long and 6ft 6in wide, it had a roof height of 10ft 6in and weighed 4 tons. It could sleep six, had a dining room and kitchen, and a bathroom complete with a toilet and running water. Its owner was Mr J.B. Mallalieu of Liverpool who set off in his mobile palace on its maiden voyage, driving from Manchester to Buxton and then on to Chatsworth at a speed of 9mph. The Austin Motor Co. built a more modest motor home

The early camper homes were often little more than sheds bolted onto a car chassis.
From the collections of The Henry Ford

A Plattenwagen.
Volkswagen AG

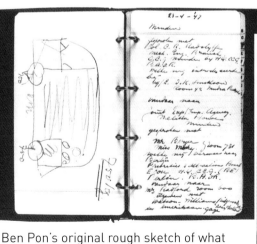

Ben Pon's original rough sketch of what was to become a world famous van.

Ben Pon – without whom the VW Camper may have never been. *Volkswagen AG*

An early Panel Va[n]
Volkswagen AG

below: The ruins of the Kraft-durch-Freude (KdF-Stadt) works in 1945.
Bill Cross/Rex Feature[s]

left: Major Ivan Hirst.
Volkswagen AG

right: Heinrich Nordhoff above his empire.
Time & Life Pictures/Getty Images

A Panel Van adapted for the German rail system.
Getty Images

below: Beetles and Panel Vans waiting to go for export.
Getty Images

below: Surf's up! Since the sixties the VW Camper Van has found a natural home beside the beach.
© *Transstock/Corbis*

above: An early Camper with a Dormobile style roof. *Volkswagen AG*

left: Early American advertising – note the second floor accomodation. *Volkswagen AG*

Rough it.

This is our Volkswagen Campmobile.
On weekends it plays. It's a cabin in the woods.
A mountain retreat. Or a cottage on the lake.
During the week it works. As a family wagon.
Delivery truck. Or both.
Any Standard VW Station Wagon, Kombi, or
Panel Truck can be a Campmobile. It's just a matter
of getting one of our Campmobile Kits.
You can get one installed in the VW you're now
driving. Or you can order a new VW with a Camp-
mobile Kit built-in.
And you can get it any way you want it.
For light travelers we have a Basic Kit. Paneling,
double bed, dinette, closets, cupboards, curtains.

For people who've been spoiled with things like
running water, stove, icebox, sink, and john, we
have a De Luxe Kit.
And for those of you who like to go Super De
Luxe, we have a Super De Luxe Kit, complete with
cabana tent, shower — the works. There's even an
upstairs.
A nice thing about any of our Campmobiles is
that the main components can be easily taken out
and put back in.
But the real beauty of the VW Campmobile is
that it does away with reservations. Packing. Motel,
hotel and restaurant bills. And tipping bellboys.
Of course, that can be rough. On the bellboys.

above: A stock advertising shot of a fine Splitty.
Volkswagen AG

below: On the assembly line in Brazil.
Time & Life Pictures/Getty Images

Crowds at Dubfest.

The Holy Grail for many Vee Dub fanatics: a beautiful Splitty in mint condition.

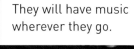

They will have music wherever they go.

Steve at Freedom Campers taking five and a brew.

Miss Lulabelle ready
for action, doilies galore.
'More tea vicar?'

A trailer to match.

It looks terminal but this
bus is a definite 'doer'.
With several thousand
pounds and hours of hard
work she'll be ready to roll.

left: A traditional
Westie interior
with the
distinctive
'tartan' fabric.

right: The high
standard of
craftsmanship in
some of today's
bus interiors
turns a Camper
Van into a little
palace on wheels.

left: One of Steve Moss's imaginative creations.

Original artwork by Steve Moss

right: Percy from Liberty Campers – the van that took me to Camper Jam.

Liberty Campers

below: The author AKA Mr Toad – in Molly. 'Poop! Poop!' *Bryan Ledgard*

for Sir Arthur du Cros who was the founder of Dunlop Tyres and also a director of Austin. It had four berths, pumped water and electric lighting, and a kitchen and a washroom with toilet. Its interior was all of the finest order, craftsman-made from the best mahogany, cut glass, leather and brass. The vehicle was exhibited at the London Motor Show in 1909 and, even though it cost £2,000 (£140,000 in today's money), a handful of models were bought by wealthy 'vagabonds'.

Other manufacturers, many of them already coach or wagon builders, began to follow suit. Duntons of Reading were one such. They specialised in ornate, gypsy-caravan-styled camper vans which they built onto a motor chassis, and the result has to be seen to be believed. Imagine Mr Toad's highly decorated Romany vardo complete with panelling and scrolling and with what looks like an Austin Twelve radiator sticking out of the front, and you will get some idea. Other companies like the Eccles Motor Transport Company of Birmingham, founded in 1913, and Bertram Hutchings of Winchester also specialised in auto homes, and soon found their vehicles were in great demand with those who could afford them.

Right from the very first, the motor home had to be exactly what it said on the label: a home on wheels. The average home on wheels owner expected a cooker, a

sink, a bed and a few chairs at the very least. The rich
owner would be looking for nothing less than a stately
home (or at least a hunting lodge) on wheels, and many
of the most expensive and luxurious early camper/
motor home conversions had winding stairs that led to a
second storey. They also boasted hot water, fitted kitchens, observation decks, electric fires, electric lights,
gramophones, radios, wine racks and masses of storage.
One pre-First World War company, Flatvan, founded
and wholly owned by ex-naval architect Melville Hart,
made very fancy mobile homes indeed, and Hart often
had them photographed outside such locations as the
Houses of Parliament to give them a little more kudos
– as if that were needed.

One of Hart's customers was the Maharaja of
Gwalior, who already owned a great number of classic
motor cars. The motor home Hart made for him was
pretty much the acme of luxury at the time. It could
sleep up to sixteen people and not only had electric
lights, a fully fitted kitchen, a stateroom, bathroom
and five-star bedrooms, but also had a separate caravan
unit fixed to a tow bar behind for the servants, without which of course no mobile maharaja's palace was
complete. It was *Downton Abbey* on wheels with a definite 'upstairs-downstairs' divide. There were separate
cabs for the driver (sometimes with an intercom) since

it was considered usual for one's mobile home to be driven by one's chauffeur. In many cases the chauffeur was also the cook since it was also considered (in the early days of British vagabondage at least) infra dig for one to do one's own cooking.

With the coming of the First World War, most English van makers turned their attention to making military and hospital vehicles, and caravans and camping vans were put on the back burner. Many of the vans were turned into mobile clinics and sent to the Western Front, and manufacturers of these vans turned to making similar vehicles as dedicated medical vehicles.

The interwar years in both Britain and continental Europe saw a massive rise in the outdoors movement, but it was mostly in rambling, cycling and climbing, three activities which were relatively cheap and accessible. Young working-class people across Europe took to the open road and the hills both as an escape from the cities and as a statement of rebellion. Many of the people in the outdoors movement were members of left-wing political parties, and at the same time a good number of them were unemployed courtesy of the Great Depression. Ewan MacColl's autobiography, *Journeyman*, paints a vivid picture of what it was like to be young in the days of the Great Depression. There wasn't much money for luxury items like camper vans, and most young people camped out under canvas or joined the newly formed Youth Hostel Association (founded 1930). Yet, though the Great Depression had crippled economies on both sides of the Atlantic, new roads were built and the motor car carried on its slow but steady incursion into all our lives. In 1925 the US government, determined to create a true public highway system, opened up the road that led from Chicago to Los Angeles, the legendary Route 66 where many (though not me) did 'get their kicks'. And by the end of the 1920s there were almost 6,000 campgrounds across America while membership of the Tin Can Club rose to 100,000.

In Britain, though our roads were nothing like Route 66 (our own equivalent, the Great North Road, still looked like it might have a highwayman lurking behind every bush), people were experimenting with home-made camper vans, building their own little dreams mostly onto the standard Ford chassis. More adventurous types converted the Austin Seven into a motor home following an article in the *Austin Magazine*. However, because of the size of the Austin Seven, this did end up as quite a small motor home – more of a 'motor kennel', perhaps. The end result was more of a botched-up temporary conversion with plywood bases for a roll-up 3ft mattress laid on top. The handbrake and gear lever did get in the way but it was reported as possible for 5ft 6in Miss Mary Pares to manage a good night's sleep in her Seven. For those who could afford them, in 1923 the Eccles Motor Transport Company of Birmingham began building motor homes on Ford chassis. With fittings including a wardrobe and dresser, a stove, washstand and tables, the Eccles motor home could sleep four people. By the end of the decade Eccles was building large luxury motor homes on coach chassis, though these were always built to order and never went into production. Individual clients travelled the world in their Eccles motor homes. One such vehicle, built on a 27-horsepower Bedford bus chassis, went to South Africa in the late thirties specially adapted with an increased capacity fuel tank (an extra nine gallons) and all the usual comforts. It toured Africa for two years before returning to Britain.

The Second World War put an end to any thoughts of camper vans and caravans, and manufacturers on both sides of the pond turned over to production for the government. When the war was finally over, even though a Blitzed and bankrupt Britain looked to be on its knees, a Brave New World did in fact seem possible. Under the new Labour government, via measures like the Town and Country Planning Act of 1947 and the National Parks and Access to the Countryside Act of

1949, footpaths were established, and, following the American example of seventy years earlier, areas of great natural beauty were designated as national parks. People once again began to look to the countryside as somewhere they could go to escape the drudgery of work, the rationing and the bombed cities to find fresh air and spiritual renewal. Most of them cycled or took the train into the mountains where they rambled and climbed but, with the coming of greater prosperity, many also began to go out into the hills or to the seaside in cars and vans, sometimes sleeping rough in them, sometimes converting them into basic motor homes. By the early 1950s, with people beginning to recover from the trauma of war and with life once more allowing for a little fun, people across Europe began to look upon holidays as a right and to regard weekends as time they could spend enjoying themselves. As more people owned motor cars, sales of caravans increased, and people who didn't want to tow their home behind them began to look for an easy-to-run small motor home that could take them away from the busy streets and into the open spaces.

There is some argument as to who made the first camper conversion based on a VW Transporter. Some experts claim that it was a Dresden VW dealer who employed a local coachbuilder to kit out a Type 2 (the vehicle has been shown at some British VW shows, it seems). However popular mythology has it that an American serviceman took his VW Kombi to the Rheda-Wiendenbrück firm based in Westfalia in 1951 and asked them to fit it with a camping interior. We don't know the GI's name, but whoever he was a medal ought to be struck in his honour, because that first conversion was the original of what would later be known as the Westie, probably the most prized of all 'stock' Camper Van interiors. Rheda-Wiendenbrück was an old established company which had started out making agricultural implements and horse-drawn carriages in 1844. By the 1930s the company had registered the Westfalia name, and was making camping trailers with room for four adults, a sleeping area and cooking and storage spaces. The unknown American who drove his newly converted Kombi out of the Westfalia factory yard that day did everybody a huge favour because, after fitting out that first Type 2, the firm saw an opportunity and a ready market, and almost immediately began producing bespoke interiors for the VW Transporter Kombi. The workmen at Westfalia were true craftsmen, and the conversion they carried out was of a very high standard. There was a cupboard for storage, curtains for all the windows, a folding table, two folding bench seats and a camping stove and icebox. Another bench seat and storage cupboard was fitted at the rear of the vehicle. The bench seats also doubled as the base for the beds, and when the whole thing was set up there was enough space for not one but two double beds. Original Westies look primitive when compared to today's luxury conversions, but for the time they were state of the art and, to people used to camping, this tin tent on wheels was a suite at the Ritz.

As well as fitting permanent, caravan-style interiors into the VW van, Westfalia also made what they called a 'camping box'. This was a brilliant piece of inspired design that was at the same time simplicity itself to install and remove. It was a wooden unit that stretched across the bulkhead behind the front seats and which, in its workings, contained a fold-out double bed, a two-burner spirit stove, a storage box and a rail for towels. The idea was that this could be slid in through the side doors on a Friday after work for the family to go away for the weekend camping, and could be taken out again on a Monday morning so the van could be made ready for its main job of carrying stuff. Comfortable bench seats were also made for the rear section, and again these could be removed.

Though the concept of a removable camping box was popular with many, it was the more permanent caravan-type conversion that proved the ultimate choice for most. As people began to earn a little more money, the Westie eventually took over the production lines and became immensely popular as a purely holiday vehicle. By 1956 there was even a Westfalia Deluxe model which had birchwood ply lining and panelling, a roof window, roof rack and canvas awning – added to which the lay-out was much improved. Thousands such Camper Vans were made, and in 1958 Westfalia was officially recognised by the VW company as makers of the VW Westfalia Camper Van, the first company to be given the official VW seal of approval. One reason for this late approval was the pop-top roof. The raised roof gave the Westie more headroom (and also could double as a sleeping area for a couple of kids). The problem was that, in order to fit the pop-top, one of the metal roof struts had to be removed. Unless the conversion was carried out properly, the structural integrity of the vehicle could be compromised, and the 'box on wheels' would no longer have the same integral strength. VW, who were jealous of their safety record, wanted to be doubly sure that safety had not been jeopardised by any alterations to the bodywork. Later on, firms like Danbury and Devon who were converting VW Kombis in the UK would be granted official VW approval for their 'pop-tops'. From 1958 onwards, even though it was carried out by an outside firm, the Westfalia conversion was included in all VW's promotional literature as part of their stable of Transporters. Year on year, as the Type 2 improved and later, in 1967, turned into the Type 2:2, the Westie interiors likewise were modified and improved – all to the same very high standard. By 1971, 100,000 Westie conversions had been installed, all 'out of house'; VW didn't make its own fully fitted Camper Van until the Type T5 in 2004.

In Britain (though there had been a few amateur DIY Camper Van conversions), the first professional VW conversions seem to have been carried out by an Austrian refugee called Peter Pitt, who in 1956 converted a Type 2 Kombi to a meticulous specification. The conversion included a wardrobe, lockers for bedding and crockery, a two-ring gas stove, interior lighting, a table with seating, a double bed and space for as many as six adults! Unfortunately Pitt then found himself running slap-bang into the implacable wall of British bureaucracy. The problem was that, even though it had been converted into a motor home, the Kombi was still classed as a commercial vehicle and, as such, couldn't be driven faster than 30mph. However, Pitt thought up a pretty ingenious way to challenge this. He drove the bus through Windsor Royal Park, where commercial vehicles were banned, and managed to get himself arrested. At the court hearing Pitt's gamble paid off and the judge ruled that the Camper Van was not a commercial vehicle, freeing up not just Pitt's conversion, but any others that might follow, to travel at normal speeds. One drawback of the ruling however was that the interior fittings had to be permanent which meant that all converted Kombis had to be examined and cleared for take-off by both Customs and Excise and the MOT.

In 1961 Pitt's firm merged with Canterbury Sidecars. The conversions they made, known as Canterbury-Pitts, are much sought after by Camper Van fans, being highly rated both for their design and for the quality of the finish. Sadly Peter Pitt died in 1969 and, because he had sole ownership of the licence, the firm stopped making campers that same year. But Pitt had paved the way for other firms of coachbuilders to follow, and the next twenty years would see a growing number of firms, from Essex to Leeds, turning out Camper Vans.

Sidmouth, on the south Devon coast, is one of my favourite places in England. It's beautifully placed in a wide, sweeping bay with an esplanade running pretty much the whole width of the bay. Like many English seaside resorts, it was originally a small fishing village that became popular for sea-bathing during the Victorian era. Nowadays it is probably best known for the great folk festival that is held there every August, when thousands of people come from all over the world to listen to wonderful music and to perform and dance, but Sidmouth is more famous amongst Camperfanatics as the birthplace of one of the most famous of VW conversions, the aptly named Devon.

Jack White was a Sidmouth builder and VW fan who bought a Type 2 van for his business in 1956. Realising that his growing family was getting too large for his Beetle, he immediately saw the potential for turning the van into a holiday home. Together with local master craftsman and designer Pat Mitchell, he installed beds, a cooker, a wash basin, a four-gallon water container, a range of fitted cupboards, a cool-box and six-volt DC electrics. With the conversion complete he drove the van over to Torquay for it to be examined by the Customs and Excise and the MOT. The owner of the garage he was leaving it at for inspection suggested that the van, which Jack had called the Caravette, be put in the window on display. By the end of the following year Jack had made and sold fifty-six Devon Caravettes, and by 1971 the firm employed a staff of seventy-five, many of them master carpenters and coachbuilders. The firm continued in business in Devon until 1989, when it moved to Durham.

The Vee Dub Camper Van story is stuffed with such characters and tales. One of my favourite stories concerns the Volkswagen Dormobile. The story goes that

Martin Walter, head of Martin Walter Ltd of Folkestone, a firm of coachbuilders that could trace its origins back to 1773, noticed that there were a great number of people sleeping in their cars while waiting for the Dover to Calais ferry. In a flash of inspiration he saw the possibility for a folding quarter-circle rooftop pop-top hinged down the side of the vehicle instead of at either end. And thus was the Volkswagen Dormobile born. Whatever the truth of the story, the name Dormobile at one time was as synonymous with the VW in Britain as Westfalia was in Germany. Together with the Devon and Danbury, the Dormobile was one of the triad of conversions given official VW approval. Quick to recognise the importance of such an imprimatur, Martin Walter's brochure proclaimed: 'Famous the world over – Volkswagen and the Dormobile Camper Van.'

The Dormobile conversions were as good as any on the market, and contained all that you would expect in a Camper Van: beds, cooker, dining table, storage space, washing facilities etc. But the most distinctive feature of all was the side-elevating roof. The most common roof conversion, before the arrival of the Dormobile, was the pop-top, where a huge chunk of the metal roof had been removed and replaced by a fibreglass top that could be raised on struts to give more headroom and sleeping space for two children. Some pop-tops went straight up, while others had either a front or rear hinge, and on average they gave a roof height, when open, of 6ft 6in. The Dormobile, which lifted from the side and was quarter round in section, gave the van a roof height of 8ft 4.5in. The roof also had a pull-out hammock on each side that could take a child or very small adult.

One gizmo the Dormobile had which the other conversions lacked was a warning light on the dashboard to tell the driver that the roof was elevated, thus saving him from leaving it swinging from a low bridge.

The firm of Danbury, who were based in Chelmsford in Essex, also made some fine conversions, and their early vans are likewise sought-after collector's pieces. They began converting Splittys in 1964 using the Panel Van as a base, which meant that the customer had to put in his own windows. There was a good reason for this: Danbury's fittings were modular and movable, which meant that the van could also double as a load carrier – not quite a Westie 'sleeping-box', but inspired by the same thinking. With the coming of the Bay Window the firm revised its design, though the seats were still movable. Danbury Bays had a full-size sink, forward-facing passenger seats, a pop-top roof and a bunk for a child that could be fitted in the cab. A 'Danbury Volkswagen De Luxe' appeared in 1977, a real luxury Camper Van with a pop-top roof holding two children's bunks, a two-hob cooker, pumped water, a cool-box, teak cupboards and drawers and a 'rock 'n' roll' bed (the rear seat swings out flat to make a base – the most popular bed form in all VW conversions).

Danbury stayed in business until the 1980s, resurfacing again in Gloucestershire where it specialised in converting imported Brazilian Bays (like Molly). The firm now works out of Bristol and supplies extremely luxurious and well-appointed Bays that look as though they come from the seventies but are brand, spanking new. There has been a major change, however: since 2006 all vehicles made in Brazil have had to have water-cooled engines. The new Brazilian Bays still have a rear engine, but they now also have a radiator, cunningly concealed behind a dummy spare wheel cover on the van's front panel.

There were many other firms that carried out Camper Van conversions, some like Moortown of Leeds, Viking of Berkampstead and European Cars of London, all converted vans with brilliant results, but none of them had the success of the 'Three D's': Danbury, Devon and Dormobile.

Nowadays there are scores, if not hundreds of firms in Britain specialising in conversions, all of them (from what I have seen) working to a very high standard. If you have the money you can buy an old VW bus, have it sandblasted and resprayed and then have it fitted out to the highest specifications: craftsman-made oak or rare wood furniture; leisure batteries; concealed lighting; electric water pumps; state-of-the-art cookers, fridges, wash basins and microwaves; TVs, DVD players and sound systems. The only limit is your imagination.

And if you want the ultimate in luxury made by VW themselves? In 2004 VW finally bit the bullet and produced their own conversion of the T5 model. Their top-of-the-range California has everything you could want, and is more like a luxury home than anything you have ever seen on wheels – added to which it can still be parked in the same space as a saloon car.

Chapter 8

Freak Street and Beyond

We're meeting Mr Miandad, meeting Mr Miandad
When we get to Pakistan in our VW camper van
We're meeting Mr Miandad, meeting Mr Miandad
It's our historical phantasmagorical destiny.

'Meeting Mr Miandad'
Neil Hannon and Thomas Walsh

Escapin' through the lily fields
I came across an empty space
It trembled and exploded.
Left a bus stop in its place
The bus came by and I got on
That's when it all began
There was cowboy Neal
At the wheel
Of a bus to never-ever land

'That's It for the Other One'
The Grateful Dead

One of the two drive shafts fell off in Swaziland. All these kids came running up, and we squatted down and looked at it hanging there. I didn't know what to do. But one little girl about nine years old was pointing to things, and her voice was so insistent that I started paying attention. She was saying that if I took a few bolts from the other drive shaft's connections, I could use them to fasten this one back on. She lived in a grass hut in the middle of nowhere, and she was right!

> *Wide-Eyed Wanderers: A Befuddling Journey from the*
> *Rat Race to the Roads of Latin America and Africa*
> Amanda and Richard Ligato

JUST OFF DURBAR SQUARE in Kathmandu is a street which goes under the Nepali name of Jochen Tole but which is known to a certain sort of Westerner as Freak Street. This was one of the major endpoints for 'the hippy trail', and it was where a good many VW buses made, if not a final stop, then a fairly lengthy sojourn.

Back in the sixties, hash was not only legal in Nepal but was amazingly cheap, and word soon spread throughout the underground network that was the hippy scene that Nepal was the place to be both for cheap dope and a hassle-free life. Thus the destination of many VW Campers became Kathmandu and Freak Street, with its German apple pie shops and its freewheeling lifestyle.

And the hippies did come, in their thousands. Some hitchhiked and some came on buses. The Magic Bus agency in Amsterdam would take you all the way there, as would Budget Bus, which left from London. You would either travel along the direct route to Delhi or via the longer way round which took in Lebanon, Afghanistan and Kashmir. In 1974 that trip cost £89 (about £400 in 2012) for a one-way ticket. Many more came to Freak Street in Vee Dubs, travelling overland across Europe and Asia and entering Nepal via the foothills of the Himalayas. Along the way they exchanged ideas and experiences in well-known hostels and hotels, the best-remembered being the Pudding Shop in Istanbul, Sigi's on Chicken Street in Kabul and the Amir Kabir in Tehran.

The overland trip to Kathmandu was long and wacky and weird, but many made it, staying for weeks and months, even years. Some of them are still there. The ones who ran the German apple pie shops and the bookshops of the Thamel (the hippy area of the city) were the sensible ones. Free they might have been, but crazy they were not; they got themselves businesses and settled down in what was then an incredibly free and friendly city. Others took to the plentiful weed like a baby takes to the nipple and many of them never weaned themselves off it. I made several trips to the Himalayas, trekking and climbing in the eighties, and remember well seeing more than a few Westerners in Freak Street who had gone so far out they would never be coming back again. Dressed like a cross between the clichéd hippy and a sadhu, they would wander the streets with a million-mile smile, their one brain cell still holding on by its very fingertips to some kind of reality. But I am running ahead of myself here. First of all we have to talk about who the 'hippies' were and what connected them with the Vee Dub bus.

To many people the VW Camper is 'that Hippy Van, the Beatnik Bus'. Hand-painted Campers covered with flowers and peace symbols, driven by long-haired freaks off their heads on hash or magic mushrooms, have been a hackneyed image in film and television ever since the sixties. Like many clichés, the truth behind and beyond the image is much more complex, and is perhaps the most interesting of all the Vee Dub stories. For not only did the van become a symbol of new movements like the Underground and the surf scene, it became, like the peace symbol itself, one of the icons of a new (or perhaps rediscovered) way of thinking. Marshall McLuhan said 'The medium is the message' and the Vee Dubs appropriated by the hippies and the surfers took the message of their tribes and broadcast them around the world, mostly to the discomfort of the establishment and settled society. You may think I exaggerate the discomfort felt by many in the face of such anarchy, but in July 2010, fifty years on from the dawning of that revolutionary decade, the sixties, the *Daily Mail*'s *You* magazine ran an article on people who used VW Campers under the headline 'Vroom with a view: Happy camper van fans on hitting the open road.' The people featured in the article were architects, teachers, lecturers, full-time mums and so on – hardly the kind of people that would run off with your daughter or burn your house down – and the piece was a collection of stories celebrating VW camping and explaining what their vans meant to the people concerned. What was most interesting to me were the letters from readers the next day. Many of them were positive, some from people who had vans, some from people wishing they had a Camper Van, and some lamenting that they had ever sold their Camper Van. Others, however, were less positive. A one-liner from a reader who describes themself as a 'Failed Mailwatch Watcher' simply reads, 'It's noticeable that not one of these people has a proper job. Says it all really.' (Architect, teacher, full-time mum – not proper jobs?) Another letter from a different reader strikes a more strident and patriotic note: 'Vile, disgusting and thoroughly un-British. You'd never catch me in one of those gypsy vans. They should be taxed off the roads. Proper people stay in hotels – not sleeping in cars like tramps. What a horrible article.' But my favourite came from somebody who signs off as 'Dude where's my town?': 'It is time that the government outlawed the overnight parking of these ghastly vehicles in lay-bys and other public areas. They ruin our beautiful countryside for the rest of us, and all because their owners are too miserable to pay camping fees.'

All these years on from Woodstock, 'Surfin' USA' and the *Oz* trial, the sight of somebody camping wild and not on an official site where their name and number and their address can be taken and logged, can still throw the petit bourgeoisie into a venomous panic. For it would seem, gentle reader, that this innocent-looking van is not just a tin tent on wheels, it is not just a compact home from home where mums and dads and kids and students and surfers and banjo players and knitters and fishermen and real-ale drinkers can taste a few hours of freedom; no, ladies and gentlemen, this van is dangerous! It has a reek of anarchy about it, even when it is being driven by an architect or teacher, and perhaps especially when it is driven by a full-time mum. And by the way, just as an exercise: the next time you are driving through the countryside, just imagine you are in a Camper Van and look out for somewhere to spend the night wild camping. You'll see plenty of small lay-bys with mounds of chippings or a butty van in them. You'll see even bigger lay-bys with lorries ranked up in them. You'll even see plenty of signs for camping and cara-van parks, but you won't see many places where you can just pull off and camp for the night. Britain is more fenced and staked off than anywhere else I can think of, and though, when I go out with Molly, I always try to find somewhere to wild camp, it is sometimes darn near impossible. I have driven mile after frustrating mile looking for somewhere off the road, a quiet spot where I can just watch the sunset and doss down for the night without somebody coming out of his house telling me that I have to move on before I bring down the price of houses in the neighbourhood, and many times I have found it damn near impossible.

But how did the Vee Dub bus come to be so strongly associated with the counterculture? And with the New Left, the surfers, the hippies and the anti-war move-ment of the sixties? It's a long story, but not too long.

First of all, let's skip back to the late 1940s and the rise of the Beat movement. In America where, unlike Europe, there were no bombed-out cities, no ruined economy (in fact the war boosted the US economy to a massive degree) the postwar society was more geared towards getting on with letting the good times roll.

There were dissenters, however. Many of the men

and women who had been to war had been tainted
with un-American ideas: they had seen Europe, they
had read books and they didn't necessarily believe that
the best way forward was to spend our way forward.
Heavily influenced by modern jazz – in particular the
free improvisation of people like Art Tatum and Charlie
Parker – and by the liberal use of the drugs and booze
that fuelled the jazz scene, the people of the new
Underground scene began to make their presence felt
in the jazz clubs of New York and in the coffee houses
and bookshops of the West Coast. They were 'hipsters'
– hip to the music and hip to the scene. Later, when folk
took over from jazz as the preferred music of the counterculture, Greenwich Village in New York City and
Berkeley, California were the coast-to-coast anchors of
the American folk music circuit.

This counterculture, as its name implies, ran slap
bang in the face of the new materialism that had begun
to explode like some kind of manic mushroom after
the end of the Second World War. The US economy,
boosted by that very same war, turned from making guns and bombs to churning out consumer goods
– cars, fridges, radios and televisions – and the advertising gurus of Madison Avenue were more than
ready to stoke the fires of the new consumer economy. Television in particular reinforced the ethos of

materialism, not just through advertising but in the way it filled the new TV screens of America with images of the perfect American family: a suburban house, car in the drive, two perfect children and the sun always smiling. The counterculture reacted to this new American Materialist Dream by creating its own more spiritual dream, along the way embracing Zen Buddhism, marijuana, LSD, Walt Whitman, Free Love, Charlie Parker, Bob Dylan, Robert Crumb, Mama Cass, Janis Joplin, The Grateful Dead and the VW bus.

Later dubbed beatniks by one journalist (after the Sputnik satellite that had been recently launched by the Russians), the Beats movement spread to Britain where it was associated with long woolly sweaters, beards, sandals and trad jazz (the women were excused beards). In the USA they tended to dress in check shirts, jeans, working men's boots and ex-army and navy jackets, much like my heroes at the time: Woody Guthrie and Jack Kerouac. Guthrie was the balladeer of America, travelling the country writing songs and poems and sketching out what he saw in a raw explosion of anger and love. Kerouac's novel *On the Road* became the workshop manual of the Beat movement. Written in three weeks in 1947, it was typed on a 120ft-long roll of tracing paper without paragraph breaks in a frenzied, stream-of-consciousness outpouring – like Virginia

Woolf on mescaline. In the novel the narrator Sal Paradise (Kerouac himself) and Dean Moriarty (based on the real Neal Cassady) make a number of road trips across America in a picaresque tale of freewheeling anarchy, meeting other Beats, hipsters, wild men and drop-outs along the way. The story rushes on in its own breakneck, crazy way, the narrator seeming at times to be delirious, not just on drugs and drink, but on life itself.

I was a teenager growing up in the smoky streets of Manchester when I first read the book, and it excited me greatly. I wanted to be like Sal Paradise, going on long journeys across the continent, meeting crazy people who had dropped out of the rat race. My own travels took me hitchhiking all over the country (even as far as London!), standing at the roadside with a sunburnt thumb, sleeping on people's floors or dossing down for the night in a park shelter. This meant that I didn't do my homework and was in constant trouble with my mother and the priests who were supposed to be educating me. I was not, in truth, a real hippy. For one thing I couldn't smoke dope – it just made me sick and dizzy – and for another, even though I had a bedroll and a blues harmonica, I always knew I had to be home for my A-levels, and that was that.

Neal Cassady, the real-life character who became Dean Moriarty in Kerouac's novel, was a Lord of Misrule who pops up later in real life doing most of the driving on Ken Kesey's Magic Bus. The novelist Robert Stone described Cassady as the world's greatest driver, saying he 'could roll a joint while backing a 1937 Packard onto the lip of the Grand Canyon'. Ken Kesey and his Merry Pranksters set off from California for New York on an acid-fuelled trip (LSD was legal in the USA until 1973) that is the subject of the film *The Magic Trip* (1964) and which was one of the prototypes of a new genre of film: the road movie. There are echoes of Ken Kesey and of Kerouac too in *Easy Rider* (1969) and *Thelma and Louise* (1991).

The hippies, the Flower Power and Woodstock generation took over from where the Beats and the Angry Young Men had left off. Though they were angry enough about things like the Bomb and Civil Rights, they were more interested, it could be argued, in tuning in, turning on and dropping out. Whatever the truth of the matter, it was both the beatniks and the hippies who took the cheap but reliable Camper Van and painted it with flowers, psychedelic swirls and curlicues and of course, the peace symbol. This benign face of the VW Camper smiled out gently on the more malign world of Nixon, Johnson and the Vietnam War.

There is no space here for a detailed look at the history of the USA in the twentieth century; all that is needed is to understand that below the expansionist, capitalist, free-market American Dream, there was always an undercurrent which ran, if not in a completely opposite direction, then at least at a tangent to the mainstream. America, after all, had been founded by men and women who had crossed the ocean to get away from oppression as well as poverty. They were not all going to lose that spirit of dissent overnight. Joe Hill, shot on a trumped-up charge, was a labour leader who has become a hero to many in the Underground, while Woody Guthrie, who wrote what should be the American national anthem, 'This Land is Your Land', was a folk singer and songwriter who had a massive influence on Bob Dylan and hence on much of the last forty years of popular music. Both men are great symbols of that other American Dream (the one that had nothing much to do with two cars in the drive and loyalty to the company).

In contrast to the hippy or Beat movements, surf culture was very focused, was mostly West Coast based and, while it had its own spirit of anarchy, the beach bums and big wave riders were less connected with political thought or any kind of 'movement'. At base, they just wanted to surf, and though at first that meant dropping out and devoting your life to saltwater anarchy on a plank, the surfing world soon became (and still is) a multibillion-dollar business with its own distinct style. However it still had (and has) something of the counterculture about it.

Although surfing had been imported into America in the early twentieth century by writers like Jack London (yes, *that* Jack London), it took off in a really big way in the 1950s and '60s and was most famously reflected in the music of stars like Jan and Dean and the Beach Boys who celebrated surfing as a lifestyle. California of course was the place to be, and Malibu its most famous beach.

Naturally enough the Camper Van fitted right into that lifestyle. You could sleep on the beach in it, the doors opened right onto the golden sands and there was room on top for a roof rack for your board.

The surfing scene even spread to Cornwall and Devon, where there is still a strong scene based around the town of Newquay. Those who so desire can go and ride the big ones and then kip in their Camper Vans supping scrumpy and eating Tiddy Oggies (as the Cornish pasty is locally known).

The VW van is still an intrinsic part of surfing culture. If you go to any of the major VW shows you will see a good few vans painted with surf scenes, with boards on top and leis hanging from their driving mirrors, and blond-haired dudes in shorts and flip-flops polishing their chrome.

Although the surf scene is an important part of the story, most people associate the Vee Dub bus with epic journeys across the planet. This is surely true for wherever the hippy trails went the Camper Van would follow, be it overland to Kathmandu or through the Americas to the ruins of Machu Picchu and on to Tierra del Fuego. There must be hundreds of books written by the travellers who made their journeys in search of themselves, and there are many stories still unwritten, or at the very least unpublished. One of my best friends, Chris, ran a tea shop in the Dales for many years before becoming a part-time university lecturer, drystone waller and archaeologist who also gives great parties. He was one of the early VW overlanders and this is his as yet unpublished tale:

'It was the summer of 1971. My friend Charles and I were both 18 and we decided to drive to (what was then) Yugoslavia for the summer. Together with Dave (otherwise known as Swanny, due to his father's unusually long neck), Charles's younger brother Harry and his friend Pete, we bought our first VW Camper Van. It was blue and white, and I can't remember exactly how much it cost, but it was less than £200.

'Although I was a couple of months older than Charles – and Swanny was in the year above us at school – Charles was the only one who had passed his driving test, so he would be the sole driver. The Camper Van could only sleep two, so we also took a tent, but there were some nights in the middle of Germany when it was so cold that we all huddled together in the van to keep warm. The van ran well as we drove through Germany, and I remember thinking as we struggled over the Alps into Austria that it was a good thing that it was air-cooled – a conventional radiator would surely have boiled dry. On we went into Croatia, eventually pitching camp on the coast at Opatija where we did nothing but eat, sleep, drink and swim for seven days. We painted some eyebrows over the headlamps and inscribed "*Stretan Put*" onto the rear bumper. We were told it meant have a nice day in Croatian . . . very hippy.

'On our way back we called in at Diano marina on the Italian Riviera where we had spent two weeks the previous summer on a package holiday. Not surprisingly the owner of a local bar remembered us, or more correctly he remembered Charles – it's not easy to forget a gangling 6ft red-haired youth. This time though we were free agents – no more package holidays for us – so naturally we set our route home via Monte Carlo, Nice, Cannes and St Tropez but we didn't stay for long – it was far too expensive.

'It was somewhere around Marseille that I learned the phrase "*le debrayage ne marche pas*" – the clutch isn't working! We eventually got it fixed okay and headed north to Brittany for another few days of relaxation, but not before dropping Swanny off to make his own way home. He had a proper job, but while he was away his employers decided that they could manage without him, and on his first day back he was made redundant – he should have come to Brittany with us!

'We would have made it home without further incident had we not run out of petrol two miles short of the ferry. At that time the cost of fuel was cheaper in England, and determined not to pay for any more French petrol, we pushed the van all the way to the ferry. Fortunately the roads around Calais are quite flat, but they wouldn't let us push the van onto the ferry so we had to buy some in the end anyway. We eventually got home some four weeks after setting off and sold the van for the same amount we paid for it – the whole holiday having cost us less than £100 each – including the new clutch!

'Our appetites were whetted, and the following

summer we decided we would drive to Istanbul. This time I would be able to share the driving. Swanny, who by then had got another job, was replaced by Neil, and for some reason we didn't buy a Camper Van – we bought a dark blue nine-seater VW crew bus – I guess it was a lot cheaper. From the outside it looked the same as a Camper Van, but in the back there were just bench seats and no fancy fittings. As it turned out it was well suited to five youths, although I don't remember the seats in the back being particularly comfy – driving or navigating was always the preferred option.

'Our route took us out via Amsterdam, where we parked the bus in a street outside an office block. We slept under the stars in the Vondelpark with a hundred or so other like-minded folk. In the morning we returned to the bus and a man in a suit appeared from the office block with coffee for us all! Unfortunately the German customs officers weren't as friendly when they stopped us on the border and made us unpack all our luggage. We looked quite a sight with all our belongings strewn around the bus. Tour buses were stopping and folk were getting off to take photos. Goodness knows what they could have been looking for, and needless to say they didn't find it. We followed a similar route to the previous year through Germany and Austria but once in Yugoslavia we carried on south into Greece. In

Athens we picked up two hitchhikers, Tom and Gerry
– a Dutch guy and an American. They'd got together a
few weeks previously and didn't seem to have much of
a plan so they tagged along with us for the next couple
of weeks.

'We hadn't seen many Camper Vans on the way but
once in Istanbul it was like Camper Van heaven. All
shapes, sizes and colours – but mainly VWs – although
I'm pretty sure that ours was the only crew bus. We
drove across the Bosphorus and spent a couple of nights
in Asia before our tent got totally wiped out in a terrific
storm. For the rest of the trip we slept either under
the stars or somewhat uncomfortably in the bus – one
on each of the three bench seats and two on the floor.
It was about this time that our hitchhikers decided to
leave us.

'On our way home we travelled through Bulgaria.
There weren't many VWs there – in fact there wasn't
much of anything – just big empty roads. We called in
at Venice, and I have vague memories of doing a conga
around St Mark's Square.

'We had a small problem descending the Massif
Central in France when the brakes failed. The handbrake had never worked, so actually stopping was a bit
of a problem. Charles, who was driving, changed down
through the gears until we were virtually at a halt, but

it was only when we crawled into a garage forecourt that we realised that no matter how slow we were going there was no way we could actually stop. It was then that I leapt out of the passenger door and ran round to the front of the bus, inserting myself between it and the fast-approaching brick wall. Fortunately I was able to stop the bus before I got crushed.

'A friendly mechanic advised us that the slave cylinder on one of the rear brakes had failed and was leaking brake fluid everywhere. He didn't have a replacement so he kindly hammered flat the brake pipe feeding the failed slave cylinder, topped us up with brake fluid and said that we should be okay driving on just three brakes until we got to the next town, provided that we were very careful. Needless to say we reckoned that three brakes were plenty to get us all the way back home safely, and it was in the middle of Paris when the other rear brake cylinder failed! This time Charles's chosen method of stopping was to drive onto a roundabout with a rather nice fountain in the middle. Our recently enhanced knowledge of mechanics enabled us to flatten the brake pipe to the offending cylinder ourselves, and we eventually made it all the way home with just two front brakes, singing a suitably adapted version of "Three Wheels on My Wagon". A couple of years later Charles bought yet another VW Camper and drove to

India, losing one of his travelling companions on the way when he was imprisoned in Iran for running over a local. But that's another story…'

Another friend, also from Yorkshire, Gordon Carr, ran a large scrapyard in Leeds back in the sixties. He was an amateur motorcycle racer and in June 1962 he decided to enter a three-day event that was being held north of Bergamo in the Italian Dolomites. Through the riders' network, he had been offered an ex-factory 650cc Triumph.

'The great motorcyclist, Ken Heanes had ridden it to gold in the International Six Days Trial. It was a heavy fire engine of a bike, but I was up for the challenge.

'An old split windscreen Volkswagen van had come into the yard – this would serve nicely for the quick trip to Italy and back, wouldn't it? Brian Swales, who had been working for me for three or four years, fancied a holiday trip as my co-driver and service team. The van was an old pale blue warhorse, and had served its time in somebody else's business, but it looked like it might just do a last turn down to Italy and back. Having the faith of the young, I looked at the dipstick, kicked the tyres, threw the big Triumph into the back and off we went blithely into a new world. The engine was, of course, the old unburstable 1200cc and the whole thing ran on a six-volt system. We could trundle down the autobahns all day at 50mph, but in those days, on other roads, we were lucky to have just the occasional bit of dual-carriageway to help us along. I don't remember the old tub missing a beat on the whole journey, so that became the start of a fond relationship.'

They trundled across Belgium and down through Germany to the Swiss Alps, making good time. 'We climbed up out of Switzerland in the dark and arrived at the top of the Grand St Bernard Pass just as the sky was lightening in the east. We flew down the Italian side and counted the hairpin bends – there were forty-two in succession. At number forty I discovered that the brake pedal didn't work any more! We were very lucky because it was early in the morning and there was no traffic about; cautious use of the handbrake and the gearbox got us down through the last of the hairpins and across the plain into the deserted, small town market square at about five o'clock in the morning. We climbed out to stretch our legs and scratch our heads. We were tired after the new adventure of all that travel, having shared the driving from the Channel ferry at Calais, and found it hard to work out what the problem was.'

They worked out what had happened later . . . 'Rarely in the UK would the braking system of a vehicle be subject to such hard and prolonged use, but thirty-nine tight bends and a lot of braking had been too much for the van's brakes. Drum brakes can generate a massive amount of heat after prolonged and heavy use and that heat can, if it reaches a critical temperature, vaporise the brake fluid in the slave cylinder; the vapour just compresses in the brake lines and won't operate the brakes. That's what had happened to our VW.

'The fluid re-forms as it cools, so things usually do come back to normal. Modern disc brakes don't suffer this problem to the same degree, and modern brake fluids have a higher vaporising temperature.'

Gordon didn't do too well in the event either, and soon realised why.

'Two hours into the first day I was beginning to realise why I was the only one riding a big bike. Mine was 650, and here a 250 was a big one; there were scores of 125s, plenty of 100s and lots of 75s and even 50s – capacity classes that we'd never dream of in England. Most of the bikes were lively lightweight two-strokes that we'd never seen. The course was largely on mountain goat tracks and steep cobbled and stepped donkey lanes zigzagging up to very high altitudes, with some rocky river crossings thrown in to slow us down. My three-hundredweight Triumph wasn't meant to be up here.

'The lunch stops were at 9,000ft. At this height my

carburettors didn't work and the engine made so little power. Like the VW, the Triumph behaved perfectly when it got back down to sea level.'

But even though Gordon hadn't broken any course records, they did enjoy the trip. 'The VW van had been so good that when it came back to Leeds, I fitted it out with beds and a cooker, and it became our first Camper Van. I put side windows in, but didn't declare that to the authorities as that would have changed its classification from "commercial vehicle" to "motor car", and thus attract a tax on its perceived value. "Rolls-Royce silver grey" paint was splashed over it – being quite forgiving, it didn't show the dirt.

'Inside I knocked up a washstand with an emergency slop bucket underneath. My wife Anne and I had three children at the time; we slept two on the shelf above the engine bay, and the other on a front seat. We shacked up quite adequately in the middle. For the next couple of years we trundled happily around England, Ireland, Scotland and Wales in it before there came another change (and child) in our lives, but that's another story!'

In 2001 Richard Ligato and his wife Amanda took their last plastic cup of water from the office cooler, closed down their computers and binned their safe jobs in California so they could go travelling in a 1978 Westfalia Camper. They put all their stuff in storage and lit out on a three-year journey that would take them all around South and Central America, and then over to Africa where they travelled round South Africa and up as far as Zanzibar. Along the way they took part in the Day of the Dead celebrations in Mexico, got dysentery and constipation in no particular order in a variety of places, had a few mechanical problems, got bitten by a monkey and charged by an elephant, and somehow managed to avoid paying any bribes, even though they had more border crossings than hot dinners.

The story of their travels, *Wide-Eyed Wanderers*, is one of the best written books on VW vagabondage you will find: it is unpretentious and informative, and written in a direct style that drew me into the narrative from the first pages:

We had it pretty good. I had a college degree, a nice home, a good job and a great wife. As long as I went to work for forty-odd years and did whatever was asked of me with a smile, I was guaranteed a good living, health-insurance and shelter from the uglier side of life.

But underneath it all I had a gut feeling that we were missing out on the calluses of life. I had a very narrow base of experience and I was watching it become narrower each year.

So they bought a yellow Camper Van from a burned-out Jehovah's Witness hippy and spent the next twelve months preparing for the journey – making sure the van was mechanically sound and getting together all the maps, injections, visas, medicines and spares they thought they would need. And then they simply went.

Reading how the mozzies almost ate them alive, how they got sick, how they had their money stolen, how elephants charged them in Africa and how the *ripio* roads of Argentina almost shook the van to pieces, you might wonder what the attraction of travelling in a Camper Van could possibly be. Richard explains it: 'That Christmas morning feeling of being alive, vibrant, thriving, pulsating, came the moment we put ourselves beyond what was comfortable, what was familiar, what was known. Once we were responsible for ourselves in almost every conceivable way, we began to feel as if we were living. It was when we took the greatest risks and relied on our own ingenuity that we felt the most alive.'

David Eccles looks every inch the teacher of English he once was. Bespectacled and studious, with long hair and a beard, he retired from teaching a few years back and now spends his life editing *VW Camper & Commercial* – one of the main VW Camper Van magazines in Europe – and organising the Camper Jam festival, one of the more recent (and rapidly expanding) additions to the VW festival world. David eats, breathes and, I would guess, sometimes sleeps Camper Vans. He has probably written more words about them than anybody else on the planet, and every one of his books is worth a read. More importantly, in the world of the Camper Van, he is one of its earliest and most adventurous travellers. His account of the trip he and his wife, Cee, made overland from Leicester to Kashmir and back is a classic Vee Dub traveller's tale. Yet, as he said to me late one night over a glass of wine while we sat in Molly at the Camper Jam, 'I can't see myself doing it now.' This, he said, was partly to do with the passing years and the circumspection that comes with age, but also with the fact that many of the countries that he and Cee travelled through on their Vee Dub Grand Tour are trouble spots in these present times. Crossing the Khyber Pass and travelling through Afghanistan in a VW Camper now would be like licking your fingers and sticking them in a light socket. Back in 1975 the world was a safer place, and it was possible, with care, for a traveller to go almost anywhere. The greatest dangers then were the weather, yellow fever, dysentery, malaria and a burned-out clutch or sticking starter switch.

Of course their families thought Cee and David were mad for throwing up good, safe teaching jobs and setting off on an overland trip halfway across the world. But when you are young, things like promotion, mortgages and pensions seem far less important, and when they saw two magpies while on their way to buy their Camper Van for the journey, they regarded that as a good omen – one for sorrow, two for joy.

They had originally intended to buy a Renault 4 van for their trip overland, having read about exactly such a trip in *National Geographic* magazine. However their plans changed when they saw an advertisement for a 1967 Canterbury Pitt Camper. Momo (they named the van after the character in the Michael Ende novel of the same name) had done little more than potter around England before, but now she was to take them across Europe and the Middle East to India.

'Our clock would be the sun . . . we had a route, places we hoped to see, but no time frame to guide us other than our own feelings.' Their route would basically follow the hippy trail across Europe to the shores of the Mediterranean and into Asia. From there they would head across Eastern Turkey to Iran and on into Afghanistan, Pakistan and Kashmir, their final goal.

They sped through Europe fairly quickly, wanting to get the 'civilised' part of their journey over as fast as possible. They realised they'd done just that when they got to Yugoslavia, where most of the roads were dirt tracks, where long tunnels through the mountains were unlit and dangerous, where bridges were often down because of landslides or floods, and where the land either side of the road was being farmed much as it had been in medieval days.

They crossed the Bosphorus by ferry, leaving Europe behind, and then set out across Turkey for Iran. It was in Turkey that they realised the real wisdom of having chosen a VW. It could be fixed almost everywhere. A sudden unexpected encounter with a massive pothole left Momo with a small amount of chassis damage and a shattered bumper mount. They stopped in the next town, asked about garages and were directed to 'the street of one thousand car repair shops'. There, three child mechanics who were still too young to shave welded the van back together again, and did it so thoroughly and professionally that the weld lasted them all the way back home. They also realised the value of the Vee Dub's air-cooled engine when crossing the deserts of Iran; even though the temperature reached 60°C and the thermometer actually burst, the engine didn't seize up. They did have a problem with the fuel though; the ambient temperature was so high that the petrol was evaporating before it could get into the carburettor. They solved the problem by wrapping wet rags around the fuel pipes to cool the petrol down.

In Tehran they decided to give Momo a complete overhaul before heading to Afghanistan and the Himalayas. Because she was a VW, the job was done and dusted (courtesy of the worldwide VW dealership) in a handful of hours, while an English couple in a Land Rover had to wait six weeks for spare parts to arrive for their vehicle.

From Afghanistan they made it over the Khyber Pass into Pakistan, then followed the Grand Trunk Road into India. They finally arrived in Kashmir, that most beautiful of lands. There they stayed on one of the famous house boats on Dal Lake, Srinagar, left over from the days of the Raj, and went trekking in the mountains. But with winter coming it was time to head for home; the route back over the mountain passes to milder climes can be closed with snow from mid-September.

On the way out they had coped with extreme heat, but on the way home it was extreme cold. The butane in the gas bottles froze, and they drove virtually non-stop from dawn to dusk with hot water bottles on their laps, chain-smoking and scraping ice from the inside of the windscreen. At one point they saw truck drivers lighting fires under their fuel tanks to thaw the diesel. David and Cee raced the winter home and made it back through Afghanistan and Turkey and across Europe just before the worst of the winter. Twenty-seven thousand miles from Leicester to Kashmir and back again, and six months later, they had to sell Momo to raise the deposit for a house. They did get another Camper Van two years later though.

They crop up everywhere, mostly when you aren't expecting it – Vee Dub travellers, I mean. I've already mentioned my old accountant, who before he swapped his beads, bong and kaftan for a suit, a Papermate pen and a double-entry ledger, was an overlander who spent more time in Marrakech than Manchester. Well, the other day yet another friend turned out to have been yet another overlander. There I was in my favourite café bar in the Yorkshire Dales having lunch and keeping myself to myself when Jane, a local lady in full bloom who was sitting at the next table, leaned across and said, 'Have you finished that Camper Van book yet?' When I told her that I was about to start wrapping it all up she said, 'I used to have one, you know – it was an old Splitty. It took me everywhere.'

Now Jane is not one of your normal Yorkshire Dales W.I. types. She dresses quite glamorously in bright colours with lots of glittery jewellery, and she also goes everywhere on a push bike, which she rides all round Settle in full mufti which marks her out a little from the crowd. Under close questioning from your ace reporter she revealed that in a previous life she used to travel the markets of the north of England from Newcastle to Bury in Lancashire, selling remnants of cloth – 'fents' they call them in these parts – out of the back of a van.

In 1966 Jane bought herself a brand-spanking-new VW Panel Van painted grey. 'I bought it in Leeds and it cost me £800 and the dealer wouldn't give me owt off even though I was paying cash.' When I pointed out that she *had* bought it in Leeds and that Leeds 'loiners' are not renowned the world over for their generosity, she still grumbled that dealers selling other makes always knocked her a few quid off. 'But everybody wanted a VW then because they were so reliable. They were queuing up to buy them, and if I didn't buy it somebody else would have given him the money, so that was that.'

For the next five years Jane travelled the markets in a Panel Van loaded up with fents, sleeping on top of the cloth at night to save herself money. 'I were damn near living in it. And it never let me down once. I even took it up to G.G. and it got all the way, loaded up with cloth.' G.G. is Gaping Gill, perhaps the most famous pothole in England. It can be found in the Yorkshire Dales, on the southern flanks of Ingleborough, and is a massive hole 110 metres (344ft) deep – you could fit York Minster inside it and still have room for several thousand Japanese tourists and an ice-cream van. Anybody who has ever been there will know that there is no road up to it; the blacktop out of Clapham turns into a rocky and rutted track, and then into a rough moorland bridleway. The only vehicles that normally make their way up there are Land Rovers and Quad bikes.

'Fully loaded?' I asked.

'Fully loaded with cloth. I was in a potholing club and we just decided to go up there one day. The weight of all that cloth gave me more traction. It went all the way, no problem.'

As well as traversing the wilds of the Yorkshire Dales, the van took Jane on holidays all over Britain, from Scotland to the deep south. But it was a trip to Norway in the van that put a little twist in the tale. Jane had gone with some mates on a potholing holiday to Bodo in the Nordland region, which is famous for its limestone cave systems. Emerging into the daylight after a long trip crawling on her belly with a lamp on her head, she noticed an interesting-looking tree root, all gnarled and weathered. 'I thought it would look great polished up, so I stuck it on the roof rack.' She took it all the way home to Yorkshire on the roof but noticed when she got back that the constant knocking of the root on the roof had made a dent in the bodywork. She could have done something with it, but 'couldn't be bothered'.

In 1970 she sold the van, which had done hundreds

of thousands of miles carrying well over its normal payload. Jane reckoned it was on its last legs and took scrap value for it. Fifteen years later, in 1985, she found herself on holiday again, this time above ground. She was in Agadir in Morocco lying on the beach in the sun when the sirocco wind came rolling in, kicking up a sandstorm that drove everybody off the beach. While sheltering in a gully called Paradise Valley, Jane noticed a grey Panel Van parked across the way that looked suspiciously like her old Splitty. 'I went over to the driver and said, "That used to be my van." He was from Yorkshire and had driven overland, going all over the place on the way. Well, he just laughed and said, "That's impossible." So we got a chair and stood on it and had a look on the roof and I showed him where the dent was.' So what had looked ready for nothing but the scrapyard had made the overland trip to Morocco without any problems. I wonder if she's still going?

Chapter 9

The Dream Goes On – Fixers and Doers and Cupcakes and Funerals

I'm cold and I'm hungry and I'm in Dundalk
I've got no bus fare, I've gotta walk
It's raining soup and I've got a fork
Where be my camper van?

'Bob Wilson, Anchorman'
Half Man Half Biscuit

IT SEEMS HARD TO BELIEVE now that the world is hurtling from one crisis of the free market to another, but there was a time when all things seemed possible, the sun did shine, the sands were golden and there were dreams to dream. 'Ha!' I hear you cry. 'You befuddled old hippy!', and 'Yes, yes, yes,' I will reply, 'Guilty as charged'. The dream of the road, of freedom, of getting away from it all was, for many of us, of course, impossible – we had kids to feed, bills to pay and stuff to look after. But there were times when we could get away and be carefree for a while at least. Although we might never be able, like Jack Kerouac, to say, 'On the road man, let's go,' at least we could 'bunk off' for a few days camping out in the hills or going to festivals. And we did, in our thousands, and hundreds of thousands – and for some of us the dream never died.

In that great world of the 'Vee Dub scene', there are now thousands of people who make a living, or who make part of their living, from keeping that dream alive: repair shops, artists, caterers, panel beaters, wedding hire firms, festival organisers, magazine editors, photographers . . . the list is almost endless. In the few years I've been involved with the scene I've only managed to meet a handful of the movers and shakers; the doers and makers, but those I have met have been quite remarkable.

Glossop is a small town on the edge of the Peak District National Park. Westwards lie Stockport and Manchester, eastwards the infamous Snake Pass and the great hills of Kinder Scout and Bleaklow. The buildings of the town are mostly built of the local gritstone that outcrops all over the Dark Peak, and the remains of the quarry workings that brought that stone out of the earth can still be seen on the hills above. A Roman road leads from the old fort of Melandra Castle, eastwards out of Glossop and on to Bleaklow by Doctor's Gate and the Devil's Dyke. There it joins the Pennine Way long-distance path. Since Victorian times Glossop and the surrounding peaks and dales have been well known to walkers and cyclists, and for the last twenty years and more the area has also been a Mecca for VW Type 2 Camperfanatics.

Glossop was also a busy place during the days of the King Cotton, and many of its gaunt Victorian mills are still standing. Still standing is one of the finest of the north's monuments to Victorian engineering: the famous Dinting Railway Viaduct which carries the main Manchester–Sheffield line through the town.

In a cul-de-sac in the shadow of the 120ft-high viaduct is another monument to fine engineering: the workshops of Alan H. Schofield, aka Classic Volkswagen Restoration Parts. The firm was established in 1988 and specialises in making panels, arches and rubber seals for the VW Camper Van – the parts that are no longer available anywhere else. It has grown from being a hobby based in a garage on the side of the Schofields' house to a family business that involves Alan and his three sons – Peter, Steven and Stuart – and the matriarch, Stephanie, the Queen of the Bacon Butty. 'Steph', like her whole family, is a VW Camperfanatic (though now she has fallen in love with a T5 which she showed me proudly round when I met them at the last Camper Jam).

You can easily find the Schofields' plot amongst the hundreds of others at any trade show. It's not just the beautiful Panel Vans decked out with the company's livery that give you the clue, nor the full-size mock ups of a Splitty and a Bay Window made entirely from genuine VW parts and Schofield's own replacement panels and seals – it's the smell of bacon butties that leads you there in the morning, and the smell of coffee and burgers at lunchtime and evening. Steph spends her time at the shows looking after Alan and the lads and the grandchildren, as well as all the friends and customers that drop in for a natter, a bite to eat and a cup of strong North Country tea or a glass of something stronger. There is an air of fun and laughter around their stall that goes well with the smells of good cooking.

Alan trained as a panel beater, and worked fitting new panels on damaged Morris Minor 1000s before starting his own business as a VW Camper Van body-work expert. He explained to me over a cup of tea and a bacon butty in his Glossop workshop that it all started off as a hobby. He and Steph and the boys (who were quite small then) were keen campers, and spent most of their holidays and weekends under canvas. Then, in 1973, almost on a whim, he bought a 1964 Splitty, a

Panel Van conversion belonging to two ladies who kept it in a garage in Poynton. Alan had heard about the van and thought that with three small boys it would be a good idea to have a vehicle the family could go camping in. He drove over to Poynton with his friend Stan to pick the van up, and then found that it had been off the road so long that they had to give it a tow start to get the engine fired up. He nursed it back home and parked it outside the house and Steph, who was used to him coming home with stuff, simply said, 'What've you bought now?'

Alan fettled the van, they bought a trailer tent to go with it, and then set off with their three boys on their first Camper Van holiday. 'The first night we slept in the trailer tent and the lads slept in the van, and the next morning the lads said, "Oh it's great in there, Dad." So we said, "Right, you're out of there then." After that, we slept in the van and they slept in the tent.' The van (and trailer tent) took them on holidays all over Britain, their favourite places being Anglesey and the Yorkshire Dales, and they still love travelling and camping.

Then there was the time the wheel came off . . .

'We were going to a VW show in Nottingham with Stan. He was in his own van with his missus Gale and their three kids. We were just going into Chesterfield down a steep hill, and the back right-hand wheel came off. So I braked carefully – if you jab at the brakes when a wheel comes off you'll go into a skid – and managed to stop the van. Stan stopped his van down the road and come up to us and said, "One of the lads told me a wheel had gone flying past us," but I didn't believe him. He's always making things up. But he were right this time.'

The kids ran down the hill and brought the wheel back. Luckily, neither the wheel nor the hub were damaged. They took one nut from each of the other three wheels, and with three nuts on each wheel, set off carefully again for Nottingham. Since they were going to a VW show they reasoned correctly that there would be some spare nuts for sale there. The culprit? A few coats of paint.

'What we discovered was that, if you paint your wheels – which we had just done – you have to tighten your wheels up every time you go out because the coat of paint wears off and the nuts come loose. Once they're a bit loose they just keep on getting looser till they come off. Everybody knows that now – we didn't know it then.'

Alan joined the Stockport and District VW owners club and dived deep into the Vee Dub world with no thought, at that time, of doing anything other than going out in his own Camper Van and having a lot of fun. Then his van went in for its MOT. It failed on the inner wheel arches, the battery tray (very common), the sills and the lower front panels both inner and outer. Alan used his years of experience as a panel beater to cut out the rusty parts and make good the bodywork. The van sang its way through its next MOT, and at a following VW owners club meeting, Alan met another member who had had the same problems with his bus. Alan showed him all the work he'd done on his own van, and the unhappy Camper Van owner asked Alan if he'd fettle his van too — so he did. That first job led to further orders and soon, realising there was a demand for his work, Alan began beating out panels on spec and selling them to owners who were handy enough to repair their own buses.

Alan was also a member of the Split Screen Van Club, and more and more people from the club began coming to him for advice and asking for panels or sills or seals for their vans. He never went anywhere in those days without at least three photograph albums of his own restoration projects, both to illustrate the parts he made and also to show how they were fitted. Seeing that there might be a future in making parts for old VWs, Alan left the car repair shop where he was working and set up on his own, working from the garage at the side of the house. He bought tools and presses and sheet-metal folders at auctions, and was soon working flat out. Ironically, one of his first major orders was for twenty cab floors for a firm of VW repair specialists – in Germany, of all places. So with redundant tools and presses from a dying British engineering industry, Alan found himself turning out panels for a vehicle created in a factory in a reborn Germany saved from destruction by a man who came from just over the hill in Saddleworth. Funny what things life turns up.

But that order for twenty floors almost did for him. 'I got tennis elbow and couldn't work the presses so I asked Rick, a friend of my youngest son, if he could give me a hand for a couple of weeks. Eighteen years later he's still here.'

Alan worked (and still does) to the very highest specification, making perfect, quality copies of the original arches and sills, the very body parts that were not available on the open market. When he began advertising in VW magazines, the panels, sills and arches started moving out of the workshop in considerable numbers. Then, in 1987, he and Steph bought the 23-window Samba, which has been with them ever since. They loaded it up with a selection of panels, sills and seals which they took down to their first ever show as salespeople and manufacturers: Dubfreeze, in Staffordshire in 1988. Once there they spread all their stuff out on a blue plastic sheet – 'we were sold out by dinnertime.'

A few years after starting Classic Volkswagen Restoration Parts, Alan realised that there weren't enough hours in the day, and that since his parents hadn't been octopuses, he also only had one pair of hands. He had several employees by then, including his middle son Steve, who was a trained VW mechanic, and they had extended the double garage to 60ft, but still they had neither the space nor the manpower to keep up with the demand. It was then that they moved to the industrial estate near the Dinting Viaduct where you can find them now.

The firm employs six people full time, and sends panels, sills and seals all over the world. The family (including grandchildren) attend every major show, and the company now has a website where you can access the catalogues for the Splitty, Bay Window and Type 25 online and order up the bits and pieces you need. Alan and Steph's eldest son, Peter, runs the website, and it is he who looks after the 'exploded' illustrations of spares that clearly illustrate exactly where the part you want for your 1957 Splitty needs to go. The three catalogues span the years 1950 to 1990, and now contain thousands of items. The firm has customers in countries all over the world, including New Zealand, Australia, the USA and Europe – wherever there is a VW owner who wants a part for his beloved bus.

Stephanie and Alan still get out in their Camper Van most weekends, though now they use the T5. At the time of writing they still had their 23-window Samba. Alan is still doing up vans for himself, and he has a current project on the go.

'I went to buy a door for a Beetle off a bloke in Harrogate and came back with a 21-window Splitty. That was twenty years ago, and I'm still working on it. Been too busy making stuff for other people.'

Sitting outside his 1995 smoke-blue metallic T4 van in the July sunshine at the Camper Jam show, boxes of 'Dub jumble' spread all around him, a beer in one hand and a freshly made bacon butty in the other, Laurence Peters is slowly and peacefully greeting the day. The van, an early 'Wedge', serves as both his bedroom and the transporter for the gear he deals in.

The main items he sells are fog lamps and spot lights, and any other VW period accessories that catch his eye. He is also the designer and importer of a superb range of retro aluminium and wood steering wheels, of which Molly for one is a proud owner.

Sitting there in the sun, chilled out and looking forward to the day ahead, Laurence is a long way physically and mentally from the social security office where he used to work, and which is now, for him, a thing of the past. No longer a civil servant, he spends his days buying and selling Dub jumble. Between May and September he covers at least two shows a month selling his stuff, and he spends the winter months collecting it.

His love affair with all things VW began when he was eighteen. One of his mates had a Camper Van in which they went everywhere until they discovered 'girls and drinking and other things', and he gave up the anarchy of the open road for a job pushing a pen in the civil service.

Then, eleven years ago, Laurence found himself thinking seriously about his lifestyle. He sat back, took a long hard look and decided he needed to change everything. 'You think that you've got used to being lied to and conned all the time, but it gets to you after a while. So, I made my mind up that I was out of there and, as I started getting over my breakdown, I decided I wanted to do something completely different. I took the money that I'd got from my redundancy and bought a Camper Van. Ever since then I've been happy – again. I'm still on my journey, but I'm loving every minute of it.'

The hardest thing, he says, is finding the stuff to sell. It's got to be in good condition. So how does he find it? He goes to a lot of auto jumbles and, like many in the Vee Dub world, he uses eBay. He also puts advertisements in local free newspapers. 'It's incredible what you come across on your travels. An old boy will give you a ring and he'll say, "Come round, I've got some lamps in the garage." Then you walk in and it's like an Aladdin's cave. He's been collecting stuff for forty years!'

He admits that at first, as a newcomer to VW jumble trading, he found himself on a steep learning curve – you have to know your 1957 front indicator lamp from your 1967 version – but he got there in the end. Now he finds that he gets a lot of satisfaction not just from selling stuff but from simply giving people advice.

He reckons that Vee Dubbers are a breed unto themselves: 'Only this weekend somebody said something to me that I've not heard before but which sums VW people up: "They are simple folk, they have simple needs. When they go away they like to look round the show, they like to have a drink and some good food with friends, they like to listen to music and they want somewhere safe to sleep with their kids." Dead simple.'

I asked him if he had ever come across the Vee Dubber's Holy Grail – the early Splitty in mint original condition up on bricks in a dry barn and covered with nothing but hay dust and a character-giving, authentic patina of chicken shit? He shook his head. 'Not yet, but I'm looking. And do you know who the best people are for helping you find stuff? Postmen. My local postie came to me one day and told me the whereabouts of four vans that had been kept under covers for two years with nothing done to them. That's how you find stuff out – from your local postie.'

Though he deals in all kinds of Dub jumble, Laurence is most proud of the classic wood-rimmed steering wheel which he designed and then had manufactured to his own specification. Full size, in polished wood and aluminium, it is a beautiful piece of kit – vintage in looks but perfectly modern in the way it works.

'I wanted one myself and couldn't find one anywhere in the standard 17½-inch bus size. So I borrowed some money, designed and specced a wheel up, and had 250 of them made. As soon as people saw them there was an incredible feedback and they went off the stall like hot cakes. That was six years ago – and they're still selling.' Since then two or three other manufacturers have copied him, but his wheel still remains the wheel of choice. So what's his next project? 'The ultimate steering wheel. Multiple layers of light and dark woods laminated together, and polished and varnished up until the wood glows and shines out at you from any angle.' I said that he'd come a long way from his nervous breakdown. He laughed. 'I love it. This is not just a job, it's an adventure.'

*

In the time I have spent working the stages of many of the theatres in these islands I have come across a good number of remarkable acts and many remarkable venues. However, none fascinates me more than the fit-up groups or solo performers who take theatre to out-of-the-way places using out-of-the-ordinary transport – sometimes even carrying their venues with them like so many thespian snails.

So it was not too much of a surprise when I found that yet that another imaginative thespian had decided to turn her VW Camper Van into a travelling auditorium. Laura Mugridge's theatre is an orange 1978 Bay Westie called Joni, which as well as being a five-seater venue, also doubles as Laura's living quarters after the curtain goes down. Her first show *Running on Air* won an award for outstanding new writing and innovation at the 2010 Edinburgh Festival, and was rated by *Time Out* as one of the best things to see. She presented the forty-five-minute show fifty times during her three-week stint at the festival, performing from the front seat to an audience who sat behind her watching images projected onto a screen stuck to the inside of the Bay's window. The *Guardian* liked her performance, calling it, 'A delightful little autobiographical show . . . you'd need an iron heart not to be won over', while *Scotland on Sunday*, giving the show a Fringe First Award, said 'It is a delight . . . it is exactly for shows like this that one comes to Edinburgh . . . it's just lovely.'

Laura Mugridge was almost born on my neighbours' kitchen table, it seems her mother was visiting friends who lived just down the road from my house and went into labour after eating one of Margaret's scones – though I didn't find this out until I actually spoke to her some thirty-one years afterwards. Once you involve yourself in the VW world you seem to find faintly unreal stuff like this out all the time.

After making her first appearance in the maternity unit at Lancaster (instead of debuting on Margaret's kitchen table) Laura lived a fairly quiet life in Kirkham near Preston until the smell of the crowd and the roar of the greasepaint drew her into amateur dramatics as a teenager. She was mostly cast in comic roles, which seems to have given her a taste for stand-up because, after studying drama and French at Hull University, she went down to Brighton and dipped her toe in the world of mirth-making, appearing at an open-mic night at a comedy club called Rabbit in the Headlights in 2005. Now, as an old comedy person myself, I would rather walk round Ecclefechan on a sleety, windy day in February with a nail in my foot than do comedy on an open-mic night. But the lass survived and went on to do more comedy in pubs and clubs around the south of England.

And yet, all the time she was doing her stand-up routines, she hankered after smaller venues, believing there was something special in a small, intimate space. Well you can't get much smaller than a cupboard, and it was in Milton Keynes, the place where, should aliens land they will immediately feel entirely at home, that she did her first one-to-one gig. Number in cast – one; number in audience – one. Heckling was encouraged.

When she and Tom, another actor and 'theatre maker', decided to get married, they asked that instead of wedding presents people should donate towards a Camper Van. Both of them had been into vans for a while and the money they collected helped to get them their 1978 LHD Bay which they acquired in June 2005. Now pretty much everybody who buys themselves an old camper finds that they have trouble of one kind or another soon after buying it (in Molly's case it was a sticking accelerator cable, a duff battery and water in the petrol tank), and Joni, who had come from France, gave Laura and Tom a fair few headaches too, most of which were eventually written into the script of the show.

They were sitting in Joni one day talking about small performance spaces and wondering where they could find a really small space for Laura to do a one-woman show – a space with enough room for maybe five people and an actor – when Laura suddenly realised she was sitting in her own best theatre. *Running on Air* took about six months to write – or 'make' as Laura prefers to call it – and was a dramatised, autobiographical road trip with Laura in the driver's seat and with whoever was sitting in the front passenger seat playing the part of Tom. 'Tom's' main job was changing the cassette tapes on cue during the show. Members of the back-seat audience were asked to read the map and were encouraged to comment on the action. At various times in the performance homemade musical instruments were passed amongst the audience and they were expected to join in. Videos of a road trip were projected onto the screen, and the whole performance was so convincing that several people got car sick over the course of the run in Edinburgh. A few people even told Laura to stop turning around and keep her eyes on the road.

'I loved working in the van,' says Laura. 'It's a magical place away from the outside world.'

The performance ran for an hour, and there were four shows a day – which is heavy going for any actor. The show went on to tour all over the UK, and is split into three sections: the first tells the story of how Laura picked Joni up from its owner in Scotland and how the Camper Van broke down several times on her journey south; the second is the story of a camping trip to

Cornwall; and the third story is all about a gig on the top of a mountain.

'Last year when I'd started writing the show I was feeling lost, and my husband challenged me to do a gig on top of a mountain. There was no audience, only three kestrels, but it was really important for me and I wanted to talk about that gig in my show. It's about celebrations, all those tiny moments.'

Never having done a show on the top of a mountain, I can't help but wonder whether kestrels heckle – or is that just crows?

Laura is now working on a new Camper Van project. This one involves a number of classic Camper Vans drawn up in a circle, covered-wagon style, and the plan is to do a different show in each one. Look out for her if you are ever at a Vee Dub show.

You might be forgiven for thinking that Lulabelle was a character from *Gone with the Wind* or was perhaps the name of a big-busted lady of easy virtue in a New Orleans bordello. You would be wrong. Lulabelle lives in deepest Yorkshire, in a place called Harrogate and, like a mobile version of Betty's famous tea rooms, she goes round festivals, fairs and anywhere else that will have her dishing out cupcakes and pots of extremely delicious tea and coffee. She is a Splitty, painted the most beautiful pink and white, and is in absolutely pristine condition. Lulabelle is owned by a young lady of true Yorkshire grit and imagination called Cathy McConaghy. Now I'm no great lover of pink, not even on my niece's Barbie dolls, but I would have Lulabelle as my main squeeze tomorrow, because she is a cracker.

As her name implies, she comes originally from the US of A, but now is happily domiciled in Yorkshire, from whence she sallies out to Camper Van dos, festivals, fairs, corporate knees-ups and children's parties, providing cupcakes on doilies, and tea and coffee served in china cups under the slogan, 'Camperlicious Catering'. Carrying her own generator and water boiler, tables and cake stands and even her own small pink picket fence, Cathy tours the country round selling homemade cakes baked with locally sourced ingredients. A recent menu included Whole Moist Orange, Chocolate and Guinness, Lime Syrup, and Pumpkin and Ginger, while her muffins came as Sticky Toffee, Double Chocolate Chip and my own particular favourite, the elastic-busting Carrot and Cream Cheese.

So how did Lulabelle come to cross the pond and fetch up travelling the country as an Olde English tea room on wheels? She began life as a simple Panel Van, chassis number 980 (which makes her one of the earliest vans to roll off the line), and began her working life as a fire truck in the town of Cochem in the Rhineland. After a long life as a red-painted fire-service wagon she was bought by a collector in Los Angeles who shipped her over to his own personal VW museum, and there she remained in the California sunshine until Cathy managed to get hold of her and have her shipped back to Yorkshire. With only 23,000 miles on the clock, her engine was in perfect condition. All she needed was a respray and a kitchen fitting inside her empty shell and she was ready to roll. In fact she was on the road and working the day after her paint job dried, the oldest working camper in existence – from fire engine to mobile cake shop in sixty years.

Before she went into the catering business, Cathy was the editor of a bridal magazine and also spent her time organising the biggest bridal exhibition in the country. But, I suppose, when you've seen one bride, you've seen them all, and after becoming bored with garters and veils and stretch limos, Cathy sold her business. With the money she got from that (plus her divorce settlement) she bought Lulabelle, fixed her up and went off in the spring of 2010 touring the offices, factories and workshops of Harrogate selling sandwiches, stews and soups. By the autumn she had worked her way into the festival circuit, and by the following year was fully established, along with other catering Vee Dubs like Chilli Gone Barmy, as one of the fixtures of the scene.

Cathy does every bit of the baking herself, sourcing as many of her ingredients as she can locally. As she pointed out, free-range eggs and local butter and milk are no problem, but ginger and Guinness are not native to Yorkshire. Tuesday and Wednesday are baking days; Thursday the cakes are packed in the van; Friday she travels to the festivals; Saturday and Sunday she works the gig. On Monday she drives home again. A fairly full week, I would have thought. She reckons that at the average festival she will shift 3,000 cakes and several hundred gallons of tea and coffee. I didn't ask her how many doilies she got through.

The pink and white van is, of course, a kiddie magnet, and Cathy does cater for children's parties, too, making it much more fun by giving the children plain cupcakes they can finish off themselves with piped icing, hundreds and thousands, chocolate sprinkles and whatever else takes their fancy – but not the Chocolate and Guinness version, I presume. As if all this hard work wasn't enough, Cathy has written a children's book in her spare time called, appropriately, *Lulabelle's Adventures*.

The VW Type 2 has ended up as many things, from fire engine to ice-cream van, from ambulance to mobile vegetable stall. Not many Type 2s have ended up as hearses and of those that have, as far as I know, only one is still working as a funeral car. Volkswagen Funerals of Coventry have it, a 1972 Type 2 hearse which has been resprayed in white to match their fleet of 'stretch' Beetle limousines and Volkswagen buses.

The company was set up by Clare Brookes and her partner Michelle Orton in 2006 to provide an alternative funeral car service to the usual black Daimler hearse with its cortege of black shiny limos. In Clare's own words: 'Having attended so many funerals and feeling lost and unfulfilled with what had happened at most of them, we decided that there must be something that can be done to help give a sense of personalisation and meaning to the proceedings and help people who find themselves in this awful position. We discussed what we would want, and being followers of the classic VW marque, and already having a wedding car hire business, Volkswagen Funerals was the result.'

Clare's family has been involved in the funeral trade for generations. Her great-uncle Jack Grimmett, who owned a taxi business, founded the firm of Grimmett and Timms as a sideline in the 1930s, turning the front room of his Coventry home into a funeral parlour. Her grandfather Arthur Grimmett joined him in the business on being demobbed after the Second World War. As a carpenter, he came in more than handy for making the coffins and crosses. With such ancestry it was natural that Clare would follow on in the business.

The hearse was originally a Pickup. It was built by VW in Hanover and shipped out to a firm of coach-builders in Augsburg with a coat of primer and minus its side gates – it was customary to do this if a Pickup was destined to be specially adapted. The coachbuilder, Fritz Freckinger, fitted it with frosted windows and a platform for the coffin and sprayed it black. The over-all effect, Clare told me, was, 'Completely hideous, it looked grim. Quite frightening in fact.' The hearse went off to Belgium where it worked in the funeral parlour of Robert Piétat before eventually ending up in the hands of a collector.

Clare bought it from the collector in 2007 and added it to her growing family of VWs (which, at the time of writing, amounted to twenty-six). She has been a 'Vee Dub nut' since childhood, and says that her first word was 'car' uttered as a toddler while pointing at the next-door neighbour's bright orange Beetle. The hearse's engine was in great condition, but the body-work and interior needed a complete revamp. The paint job was done by the famous Charlie who did the paint job on the Splitty in the film *Camper Van Crisis*, while the interior work was done by Clare herself. One of the first jobs the hearse did was take Clare to her own wedding. She sat in the front with the chauffeur while the part normally reserved for the departed was filled with flowers.

Since that happy day it has mostly been used for funerals, which, as Clare says, though obviously not the happiest of affairs, are made much more bearable (for some people at least) because the hearse is white, the colour of peace and rebirth. The company may be based in the Midlands, but it offers a nationwide service, and transports the hearse on a lorry to wherever it is needed. Since rolling off the assembly line in Germany, the van has done a total of 40,000 miles – for a flat four air-cooled engine that means it is hardly run in.

All kinds of people have used the service, from people who simply want a brighter, more cheerful send-off, to the usual suspects: the VW fanatics. The hearse has a roof rack, which over the years has been used to transport many things. One customer, a model aircraft enthusiast, had a five-feet wingspan model aeroplane escort him on his final drive, but my favourite is the surfer who had an ironing board accompany him when he finally rode the Big One. It seems he was not the world's greatest wave jockey, and his fellow surfers down on the Cornish coast would often shout out to ask him teasingly where his ironing board was.

*

The village of Clapham in the Yorkshire Dales is one of the bonniest villages in England, home to the Ingleborough Cave Trail, a very fine wool shop and is now the home of Freedom Campers, one of the newest additions to the world of Camper Van restorations. When we talk about restorations, we are not talking about a bit of a welding job here and a new door handle there; we are talking about back to the shell, hack out the rust, sandblast the rest, weld on the new – and all of this followed by a complete new paint job. A restoration as thorough as this could take anything up to six months per vehicle and doesn't come cheap, but at the end of it you have an as near as dammit perfect bus that will last you years.

Freedom Campers was set up by Steve Domeney and his partner Helen Venus, co-owners of Doris, the only Cave and Fell Rescue Camper Van in the world, a blue and white Late Bay which transports them and their two border collies on holidays as well as on rescue call outs (Steve is a member of the local team). Steve's love of the mountains, together with his love of the VW Camper Van, began when he was stationed at RAF Brawdy (Welsh: Breudeth) in Pembrokeshire, which Steve describes as Wales' best kept secret. He was trained as a weapons engineer, and as such was responsible not just for working with armaments but with the peripheral mechanics too. As he explained, if you've just armed a missile, you don't want the hydraulics that are lifting it into the plane to be faulty, so you end up doing a lot more than is in the job description. He was not a great fan of authority, however, and his attitude didn't endear him with the brass hats, which meant he did more than a few tours of duty in Northern Ireland and the Falklands.

It was while he was in the forces that he began tinkering with classic cars. His first restoration job was on a Sunbeam Rapier ('wish I'd kept that one') after which he moved on to MGs and then Vee Dubs, both Beetles and buses. He eventually came out of the RAF and went on the road as a field engineer, travelling 50,000 miles a year plus.

'I just ended up being a stress head, sitting there in the outside lane doing ninety trying to make your next appointment. But then, at weekends, you'd get in the van and it would all melt away – pottering along in the inside lane doing fifty. Vans are bloody brilliant.'

By then Steve had been fixing up VWs for years, and when he was made redundant for the third time, he and Helen took the redundancy money and put it into the business. They'd originally intended to set up a holiday Camper Van hire firm but they found that they had to put that side of the business on the back burner. While bringing their own vans up to scratch for hire they attracted the attention of fellow Camper Van owners who began bringing their own vans in for restoration, and as Helen says, it all snowballed from there.

They no longer do running repairs and now concentrate on complete rebuilds. When they started they did take in repair work but, as Steve said, they found that all too often they were expected to fix other people's botched-up jobs. Some of the vans didn't need repairing, they needed resurrecting.

So far they have done fifteen full restorations, and they do everything from bare metalwork to needlework. The one thing they don't do is the curtains. Helen, as well as being the boss of administration and publicity, is also officer in charge of sandblasting and spray painting – Steve reckons that she's better than him at both those jobs. Being a woman, Helen has no problem multitasking, and as well as being a bodywork specialist she also freelances in marketing and leads groups of people on walking holidays.

In the workshop when I visited were a 1965 Splitty LHD in for a complete restoration including conversion to RHD and a 1969 Early Bay also in for the full Monty. Both of them were California imports and had very little in the way of serious rust problems. The Early Bay, however, was once somebody else's project until he ran out of time and money, 'So what we have is a partially restored shell and a lot of boxes with stuff in. It's like a massive jigsaw.' Both the Splitty and the Bay have customers waiting for them.

'We go to an awful lot of shows,' Helen explains, 'to see what's going on, to get our name about and to meet lots of old friends. And we're also members of the Late Bay online forum [www.thelatebay.com].' The Late Bay forum is not a club but a loose collective of like-minded individuals who have a common interest in the model. You'll find everything posted up there, from requests for information on camping sites near the National Cycling Centre, to postings from people who've had their buses stolen. As the buses have increased in popularity and price so thefts have gone up. The club also have informal meets. Steve and Helen organised a Halloween Spooktacular in the Dales, and dozens of Dubs turned up for a night of witches and wizards, vampires and camp fires. At the time of writing, another meet is scheduled for Gordale Scar. That would be something to see – all those Late Bays with the wonderful backdrop of that great limestone gorge.

Helen reckons that the spirit of the sixties still runs through the whole scene. 'There are lots of people who were children of the sixties who still have vans, but there are also lots of people who are their children and who grew up going out in Camper Vans, and now they've either got one of their own or want one of their own.' She did wonder at first whether the present boom in the Camper Van was going to last but, as Steve says, it's a classic model, and there are lots of spares available so it's possible to keep one running pretty much for ever. So, like all classics, it looks like the Vee Dub Camper will be around for a long while to come. Just before I left the workshop Steve said, 'One thing we haven't talked about is the sheer joy of working with these vans. They are simply amazing.'

Steve Moss runs a company called Splitscreen Innovations. You'll often see crowds round his stall at the Vee Dub shows because he is the man who put the beautiful Splitty in the London Underground. The alchemy he brings to bear on his photographs produces images that are simply amazing: solarised buses loom out of a desert landscape with a starburst sun in a surreal sky and, as mentioned, Camden Town Tube station has, not the usual underground train, but a gorgeous red and white Splitscreen bus pulling the carriages.

I asked him how he got into the business of making Salvador Dali Vee Dub art and he told me that he'd spent much of his working life as a mechanical design engineer for a large bus manufacturer mostly involved in the design of bus chassis. He'd been a Vee Dub fan most of his life and had at one time owned both a Splitscreen bus and a Bug. After working in both the USA and Australia he came home, and as he says, 'just started tinkering with all these photographs I had'. Based in Camden Town (hence the Tube photo) Steve uses Photoshop software to manipulate the images then prints them onto Fujichrome crystal archive paper which will last 150 years if kept out of direct sunlight. Each image can take him four hours or so of work before it's ready for printing, and Steve sells his pictures both at VW shows and through his website. His latest project is a VW Camper Van Dalek, which at the time of writing was still a work in progress and had taken him forty hours.

I don't know if anybody is specialising in VW midwifery, because if they were that would mean you could be hatched, matched and despatched in a VW. There is, as far as I know, only one VW funeral service, but there are plenty of companies specialising in VW weddings. Not only is a Camper Van, particularly a state-of-the-art Splitty in full concourse livery, a great-looking van, transporting the bride in a large bus means that she gets to the church with her dress and veil uncrumpled.

My nearest Camper Van hire firm, Liberty Campers of Otley, don't just offer classic campers for hire in which you can roll off into the Yorkshire Dales for a holiday. They also offer a wedding vehicle in the shape of a beautiful two-tone Splitty called Dylan.

I was due to set off for Kamper Jam in Molly, everything was packed and I was really looking forward to the weekend when the garage where I'd taken her for a simple service rang to say that there was no way she would be out of the workshop that weekend, or the weekend after; Molly had a major problem with the fuel injection system and it couldn't be solved overnight. (In the end it took two weeks to fix and I only solved it by binning the fuel injection system and putting Weber twin carbs on her, but that's another story.) So there I was – stymied. A friend recommended that I ring Liberty Campers and when I explained the problem to John and Tracey, who run the firm, John just said, 'Come on down and you can take Percy for the weekend'. And that's exactly what I did and I had a terrific weekend thanks to Percy and Liberty Campers.

And that, in my experience, is the kind of helpfulness and generosity you find throughout the Vee Dub scene. Many of the photographs you see in this book wouldn't have been possible but for Percy, a four berth Bay in dark green with psychedelic swirls and a fine companion over that sunny weekend; others in the fleet are Dougal, an orange and white Bay Window like Molly; Daisy is white all over with a spattering of flowers. Dylan, the wedding bus, is a beautiful state of the art Splitty while Poppy is an old lady Westy more than forty years old and Brian is a green Devon nine years young who, like Molly, came off the Brazilian presses; Liberty is the new kid on the block, a red T25.

John and Tracey started the business five years ago after John was made redundant (how many stories of VW businesses have a similar beginning?). They'd had Dylan for a few years and were really into the VW and camping world so it seemed natural to spend their money on a fleet of vehicles and do something that they both enjoyed. They were also lucky in that John was trained as a mechanic with a special knowledge of Vee Dub engines. This has meant that he's been able to keep on top of the maintenance side of things, so that even though the vans in the fleet are mostly old buses they run like sweet young things.

The wedding hire is busy throughout the year but as you would expect the camper van hire tends to be seasonal with most lets running from March to October. People who hire the vans for the weekend tend to spend their time wandering about the Lake District, Yorkshire Dales or the North Yorkshire Moors and Coast; Otley is ideally placed for all three. Longer hires take people further afield into Scotland and the Hebrides. Because the vans are so well maintained they have never had any major troubles ('Touch wood' John says) and beyond a few scratches and bumps they've had no problems with the people driving their buses.

'You know what Vee Dub people are like,' said John, 'They're great characters, outdoors people mostly and they respect the vans and love driving them.'

There are so many other characters on the Vee Dub scene who are living the dream, keeping old VW fire engines and ambulances alive; fitting bespoke, hand-made and beautifully crafted interiors; editing magazines, keeping clubs like the Split Screen Owners Club alive or running massive spares warehouses like Just Kampers or VW Heritage – I could have filled a book with their stories alone. And when it comes to other uses the VW Camper Van has been put to the story goes on.

Suffolk singer, Peter Hepworth found a 1962 Splitty rotting away in a ditch and turned it into a solar-powered mobile festival stage. He bought it from the farmer whose ditch it was deteriorating in for £4,000 and brought it back to life. Peter kitted it out with a stage that can be assembled in front of the side doors with speaker stacks and lighting rig around it. The system is powered by solar panels on the van roof which charge a rank of leisure batteries giving Peter a respectable 2 kilowatts of sound. He has insured it for £30,000.

And there you have it, one more story amongst so many. Check out the hot dog and chilli stalls, the mobile discos and the ice cream vans at the Camper Van festivals; have a long good look at the working pickups, the ambulances from Germany and Holland and you'll find that all of them are the lovingly nurtured vans of some really interesting people.

Chapter 10

Tailpipe

Johnny go tell your old man
We're taking out the old splitscreen
The weatherman says the storm has passed
And the ways are open and clean

'Splitscreen'
howdenjones

SO, HAVING FED THE RAT with a 2001 Brazilian orange-
and-white Bay called Molly and now having come to the
end of the book, how it has been? Has the old girl lived
up to all the fantasies or has it been marred with what
psychologists call 'the melancholy of attainment'?

Well, life with Molly has been a learning curve for
both of us. The journeys we have made over the last
years haven't been the subject of any road-trip book in
the style of *Travels with Charley* yet (though an idea is
smouldering in one of the dark cupboards at the back

of my mind, something to do with old country pubs
perhaps) and, as in any marriage, we've had our smooth
times and our rough times.

The rough times were mostly the result of one particular cowboy mechanic making a mess of the poor old
girl's innards. If you want to find a good VW workshop
join your local VW bus club and ask them. I didn't. A
bloke I met in a pub told me about 'this bloke' he knew
who had a VW workshop down the back of the back of
the back of somewhere. Never buy anything in a pub
except beer and pork scratchings. They are not good
places to buy 'stuff' because it will mostly have fallen off
the back of a lorry. Pubs are also not good places to find
specialist vehicle repairers.

So on a rainy November afternoon I left the orbital
motorway that circles Manchester and entered the
Bermuda Triangle of the city's hinterland. I threaded
my way through a maze of half-demolished streets and
boarded-up factories until I came to a land of chain-link
fences, slavering guard dogs the size of wolves and hand-
painted signs telling me that this unit took in any kind of
scrap while that unit specialised in pressure hoses and
yet another was devoted to doing stuff with pallets. The
metalled road had turned into a cinder track scabbed
with pools of oily water and, with killer wolves batter-
ing the chain links either side of me, I chugged along the

track in Molly, until I drove through the gates of a der-
elict factory into a yard filled with VW Camper Vans in
various stages of dying. All that was missing was David
Jason as detective Jack Frost in his raincoat and trilby.

A man cleaning his hands on a bunch of waste cotton
smiled and told me she'd get a complete engine overhaul – new piston rings, valves, grommets, push rods
and pull whatsits, and a twin carburettor which would
make her 'pull like a train' – and she'd be ready in three
or four days' time. Six weeks and more than a thousand
pounds later I drove Molly coughing and spluttering
back towards the Yorkshire Dales a sadder and poorer
man. We got as far as the Lancs/Yorks border on a night
of rainstorms and heavy traffic and coughed to a stand-
still under Pendle Hill. Pull like a train? The bloke must
have meant 'bridal train'. I travelled home in the cab of
an AA tow truck with Molly cranked up on the truck
bed, and the problem turned out to be bugs in the fuel
system induced by the same cowboy. Never again will I
listen to blokes in pubs, unless they're playing the banjo.

Over the years I have hung a few things on Molly
like extra spot lamps, and I have had the original accelerator linkage modified so it no longer looks and feels
like something Heath Robinson would have been proud
of, and now she runs and looks just fine. My grandchildren, Toby and Felix, and their friend Lizzie covered

her with flower transfers and inside she's done up like a fortune-teller's caravan with Indian throws and cushions so that, as an old hippy, music-making folkie, I feel quite at home in her. There's space for my Orvis Travel Rod and my mandolin or my short-scale neck banjo, and she's taken me on many a trip to the riverbank and folk festival.

Many of my travels with Molly have been short camping trips, fishing for brown trout on the Eden and sea trout on the Lune, and there is something really wonderful about waking up on a clear summer's morning with the sun just coming over the hill knowing that you can put in a good hour on the water before breakfast. And it's just as good knowing you can fish on into the dusk, sometimes getting the best rise of the day as the big sedges hatch on the water and the fish go wild for them.

And what of the future for Molly and I? Well, I'm determined that I'm going to take her over to Ireland for the fishing and the craic; I've lots of old friends all along the western fringes of that country that I haven't seen for far too long. I also want to tour the Highlands and Islands of Scotland for pretty much the same reason. I love the Marcher Country of the Welsh Borders too, so I aim to spend some time tootling round Ludlow and Shrewsbury and Bishop's Castle. I've been thinking for a long time about working on a book on Churchcrawling – and Molly would be the ideal companion . . . so, there's still plenty to go at – and of course there's always that book on the great country inns of Britain, the research would be fun.

I've trundled round the folk festivals in Molly too and that has been a great delight. I remember watching a wonderful band called The Outside Track at Fylde Festival then wandering into the bar to find two old mates from the Irish sessions round Preston and Appleby fair, Tom Walsh the melodion player and piper and Hugh O'Donnell the fiddler, dressed like Mafiosi or horse traders (there's not a great deal of difference) lashing away into a great set of reels. The banjo came out and several hours later I made my way towards Molly, head still spinning with the jigs and the reels. I must have had all of twenty yards to go but I still got a bit lost. I think it was the medication I was on.

A fellow folk musician I met in a pub told me another Camper Van story recently – perhaps the best one yet. The musician is a friend of mine called Sean Halfpenny and the pub was a good traditional Irish pub in Connemara called E.J. Kings. Sean is a bodhrán player and singer who, though of Irish stock, spent many of his formative years 'across the water' in England. As a young musician he found himself living in East Anglia and playing in a band called The Suffolk Country Band who were busy enough playing a mix of Irish and English folk in folk clubs and village halls around Suffolk and Norfolk. The band bus was a late Splitty with (and this is very important) a roof rack along the full length of the top.

The group were driving back on a raw winter's night from a gig near Bury St Edmunds. Snow lay everywhere and the roads were iced over. 'We were coming down the only hill in the whole of East Anglia, and were doing OK, perhaps too OK because we got a bit complacent. I expect we drove a little too fast down that hill because we suddenly hit the verge, ran up it a bit and then the van flipped over, completely upside down on its roof. Instruments and musicians went flying and we found ourselves lying on the roof (now the floor) as the van shot off down the hill.

'It was sliding down the icy road like a sledge on the "runners" of the roof rack. There was nothing we could do but hold on and hope we didn't hit anything. At the bottom the road curved to the right and there, on the bend, was an old country pub. We shot straight across into the pub car park. There was an almighty row as the steel runners hit the blacktop and we shuddered to a halt without having hit any of the other cars parked there.

'The whole pub ran out and dragged us out. We had a few bruises and were all shaken but nobody was badly hurt and, more important, the instruments were OK. In the morning a gang of the local lads came round and heaved the van back onto her wheels. Beyond a few dints and bumps she was right as rain, started up first try and we drove off in her. No harm at all . . .'

A Camper Van, in other words, is built like a bus, and as you would expect, that's just how Molly handles, and a vintage one at that (the design is forty years old after all!). But she is mighty fun to drive and there is something really pleasurable in sitting high up above the road, trundling along at a steady fifty-five miles an hour taking in the scenery all about you through her big bay window. She's sluggish on hills but she always gets there in the end, and with food and drink in the fridge and the gas bottle full there's no need to worry about finding somewhere for lunch. Lunch, dinner, afternoon tea – can be wherever you want it.

Another great thing about a van like Molly is that she can be parked in a normal car space, so I've been able to sneak her into tight little corners in all kinds of places: round the back of a pub or three, behind the stage at festivals and snuggled in under the trees on many a riverbank and lakeside. She's particularly handy at taking me to folk sessions in country pubs, and it's great being able to toddle across the road with the mandolin and join in the music.

Toddling back to the van is a different matter, and I now make sure that the bed is made and that everything is set up for the morning. I also make sure I have a torch so I can find my way back. There have been times when I've wondered whether it might not be wise to tie a ball of string around Molly's bumper and tie the other end to my belt so I can find my way across the field in the dark. But I soon realised that if everybody did that we could all end up tangled together in the middle of the field in a giant's cat's cradle, all lost, wet and muddy waiting for the Fell Rescue team to come and cut us apart.

I haven't kept a journal of our travels yet but there are certain golden times that have lodged in the old noodle as very special. A tubby, overall-wearing Chinaman once said that 'a journey of a thousand miles starts with a single step'. It can also start with the turning of a key in the ignition. One frosty October morning I'd decided to just go where the day took me. I like that kind of travelling, the random venture out of doors, the kind of thing Mole does in *The Wind in the Willows* when he chucks down the limewash brush, mutters, 'Hang spring cleaning', and trots off into the outside world with not much idea of where he's going other than – out there.

Loaded up with food and water, a new gas cylinder and a full petrol tank I turned the key, Molly roared into life and off we went in the general direction of the Lake District.

Traffic was light on the road to Kendal and as I rolled along I took the turn-off for the Furness coast, no thought in mind other than to see what lay ahead. The sun was well up by now and the frost and early mist had cleared and it looked as though it was going to be one of those strange almost summery days that mid-October sometimes brings. An hour or so later I was on the fringes of the Lake District, heading down the Furness peninsula. The trees were turning with the year and the hills were blanketed in gold and rust and copper. I tried to describe the colours of autumn in a poem once and came to the realisation that words can get close but will never quite make it.

And all the trees turn fires and precious stones,
Are tigers' eyes, cornelians, jasper and topaz,
Leaves leap, tin fish they rust and swim from trees . . .
fools gold,
Parrots' feathers, lemons and oranges,
Egg yolk, clowns' noses, pips from the sun.

I hauled off the road at Cartmel and pulled into

the car park at the Priory, made myself a coffee then slung my camera on my shoulder and walked across to the church. Cartmel is one of my favourite northern churches, with interesting stained glass windows, some of the best misericords in the country, and a large collection of skull and crossbone flagstones. From Cartmel I headed west, thinking that I might find somewhere on the coast where I could park up for the night. I rarely go on authorised camp sites. Wild camping appeals to me far more and, though it's difficult to find spots away from the crowds, I've mostly managed it, and there's nothing better than waking up in the morning on the banks of a river or lake, catching the morning rise before the other fishermen are about.

I'm always looking out for likely stopping places even when I'm in the car, but next time you are out for a drive in the country, see if you can spot places to stay – not lay-bys or camping parks but wild places on the moor's edge or near a beach or a forest. I think you'll be surprised at how hard it is to find places to stop. England must be more fenced and circumscribed than any other country in Europe, and wild camping is getting more difficult by the year. Much of this is to do with the way New Age Travellers were turned into folk devils a few years back and the police got more than a little heavy handed when it came to moving people on. It's funny how the sight of a certain kind of van can bring out the worst in some people.

I remember getting lost down a lane near Silverdale close to Morecambe once. I was looking for a spot to park Molly for the night that was free and wild and not near anybody else but had found myself trundling down a narrow road that seemed to end in a cliff drop. There were a number of houses along this road and as I made a fifteen-point turn in its narrow confines a Mr Pooter (*Diary of a Nobody*) came out of his house red of face and sure of rights.

I stuck my head out of the window. I had very long hair at that time and was wearing a striped sweater so I definitely did not look like your average *Daily Mail* reader. 'Don't you know that this is a private road?' he spouted at me in best dole office clerk fashion. I said that I didn't but that I would be gone as soon as I could get Molly turned about. I put her into reverse and began the fourteenth of my fifteen-point turn. As I was straightening her up to leave she gave a jerk, her little engine gave a cough and a lurch and then died. The best thing, as I knew well, was leave her for a few moments to sort herself out and she would be as right as rain.

I shrugged. 'Looks like I might have to stay here.'

'But you can't stay here!' On the Farrow and Ball

shade chart his face had gone from Rose Pink to Righteous Puce.

'Well it seems I might have to. She often does this. If I leave her overnight she'll probably start up again.' He stared at me, speechless. 'There is one thing we could try: You could give me a shove and we can see if she'll go on a push start.'

And he did and she did and I laughed my way out of Silverdale and its ever-so-friendly Little Englander.

So that October day I left Cartmel with high hopes of finding somewhere bonny along the coast to park up for the night. A couple of hours later, having scoured the coast in vain, I found myself in the environs of Barrow. Now as somebody who once described Barrow as a town on the end of a ninety-mile-long cul-de-sac I did not want to find myself spending the night there in a Camper Van. Barrovians have long memories.

So I turned round and headed back; I hadn't noticed how the day had worn on and the sun was now heading well into the west. I put my foot down and hammered back along the coast road the way I had come until I found a road that took me into Grisedale and the forest. I used to come here years ago when a great character called Bill Grant ran the lovely little Theatre in the Forest there, a small place that seated about a hundred, but made up in atmosphere what it lacked in numbers. I had many a great night there; I don't know who enjoyed themselves the most, me or the audience.

The tourist season, like the day, was drawing to a close so there were only a few walkers and cyclists making the most of the autumn sun. I drove on through the Forest Park Centre and climbed further into the hills looking out for a place to stay. I'd almost given up when I noticed a track leading into a picnic area. I swung off the road and parked Molly right at the far end where I would be no trouble to anybody, set out my water and waste containers, put the kettle on, switched on Radio 4 and watched the sun go down.

There wasn't a soul about, just me and Molly and a BBC voice telling me that it would be a frosty night. On the edge of light a small herd of deer came out of the forest and crossed the clearing, vanishing again into the trees on the other side. They ignored the van completely. A tawny owl landed on one of the picnic tables and stared at me for a while before launching into the air again on its great soft wings. With night closing in I stepped out of the van to go for a pee and looked up at the sky. Standing there with no light pollution from houses or city street lamps I could see that the sky was ablaze with stars that looked brighter and somehow nearer. Accepting the mystery I went back into the van, drew the curtains, made the bed and, book in hand, slid beneath the sheets.

The next morning I woke with the sun fingering its way through a chink in the curtains. Stepping out I saw that the hill I was on was islanded in a sea of mist, and across the valley other wooded gold and copper islands rose out of the milky, swirling sea. By the time I'd finished breakfast the sun had burned the mist off and I trundled through the Lakes to Langdale in bright sunshine.

Notes

p1: 'a sealing-wax red, Splitty Panel Van'. Until the Bay Window arrived in 1967, all VW vans had split screens, hence the nickname 'Splitty'.

p42: 'On January 1st 1948'. *Ivan Hirst — British Officer and Manager of Volkswagen's Postwar Recovery* by Ralf Richter (Volkswagen AG, 2004).

p43: 'Yes, that is as it is seen by the world perhaps'. Richter ibid.

p44: 'We had to build it by hook or crook'. *Volkswagen Transporter: The Legendary Type 2, 1950–82* by Laurence Meredith (Crowood Press, 1998).

p55: 'Soon given the nickname "Samba"'. The word Samba seems to have been coined by VW largely because they felt that calling the bus after a modern Latin American dance, reflected both their new interest in Brazil and also the VW's hip and trendy status.

p71: 'one country stands out above all others: Brazil'. My own van, Molly, is a Brazilian import, an air-cooled model produced a couple of years before the factory, in compliance with new emission laws, began producing water-cooled engines only.

p78: 'The VW bus stands in a class of its own'. *Volkswagen Transporter*, Meredith.

p81: 'no longer happy or smiling'. Ibid.

p87: 'Thousands of tired, nerve-shaken'. *Our National Parks* by John Muir (Houghton, Mifflin and Co., 1901).

p90: 'Tin Can Tourists of America'. The British Camping and Caravan Club was founded in 1907, though for sixty years the club looked down its collective nose at the motor home, only admitting owners as members in 1967.

p92: 'all in great comfort and at a price you can easily afford'. I'm not sure about the last claim, since a skilled worker in the mid-1920s would be lucky to earn much more than $20, then the equivalent of £4 a week – that's if he was working. The Kampcar would therefore have cost him more than half a year's wages.

p104: 'By the early 1950s'. Strange as it may seem, my first job at age fifteen included Saturday morning, which you were expected to work. With church taking up much of Sunday there wasn't much time left for fun. No wonder people soon dumped both 'half-day Saturday' and the church-going.

p126: 'the Wobblies'. International Workers of the World – a labour organisation that sought to bring peace and equality through the union of working men and women across the planet. Nobody knows why they were called 'Wobblies'.

p128: 'the Beach Boys celebrating surfing as a lifestyle'. In some way that is still a mystery to many, Hawaii became the fiftieth state of the USA in 1959.

p139: 'The story of their travels'. *Wide-Eyed Wanderers: A Befuddling Journey from the Rat Race to the Roads of Latin America and Africa* by Amanda and Richard Ligato (Pop-Top Publishing, San Diego, 2005).

p139: 'the *ripio* roads'. The surface of the dirt and gravel roads of the Argentinian outback are corrugated across the line of travel. The wind, ice and sun have produced a series of deep ruts a few inches apart that loosen every nut, bolt, electrical contact and fuel and brake pipe. These roads run for hundreds of kilometres. 'The only answer was to drive like a madman.' Ibid.

p145: 'fents'. Fents are the ends of faulty runs in the mill. When the fault is in the middle, the mill, unable to sell the whole bolt of cloth, cuts out the fault and sells the rest as 'fents'.

p152: 'bacon butty'. Bacon butties and sausage butties are the 'food of kings' at the shows.

p156: 'dinnertime'. Lunchtime in the south of England and midday in the rest of the world.

p171: '*Camper Van Crisis*'. *Camper Van Crisis* is a superb documentary about a Camper Van being rebuilt from a virtual 'scrapper' state in time to take part in drag races at the Santa Pod racetrack. They have only 150 days to manage it, but they do.

p180: '*Travels with Charley*'. John Steinbeck set off to explore America in a motor home accompanied by his dog Charley in a bitter-sweet journey 'in search of America'. Though Steinbeck didn't journey in a VW the book is a classic of travel writing.

p185: 'Churchcrawling'. The relatively harmless pastime of visiting churches in order to examine the carvings, tombs, misericords, stained glass and other glories they contain. It does require a small amount of crawling and the author has crawled his way into a number of small books on the subject.

p188: '*And all the trees turn fires and precious stones*'. 'Autumn Dentdale' from the book *Buns for the Elephants* by Mike Harding (Viking, 1995).

Index